# LIFE OF

# Ven. Padre Junipero Serra

WRITTEN BY

### VERY REV. FRANCIS PALOU,

Guardian of the Convent of San Fernando, Mexico.

---

TRANSLATED BY

### VERY REV. J. ADAM.

---

*SAN FRANCISCO:*
P. E. DOUGHERTY & CO., BOOK AND JOB PRINTERS, 412 COMMERCIAL STREET.
1884.

Windham Press is committed to bringing the lost cultural heritage of ages past into the 21st century through high-quality reproductions of original, classic printed works at affordable prices.

This book has been carefully crafted to utilize the original images of antique books rather than error-prone OCR text. This also preserves the work of the original typesetters of these classics, unknown craftsmen who laid out the text, often by hand, of each and every page you will read. Their subtle art involving judgment and interaction with the text is in many ways superior and more human than the mechanical methods utilized today, and gave each book a unique, hand-crafted feel in its text that connected the reader organically to the art of bindery and book-making.

We think these benefits are worth the occasional imperfection resulting from the age of these books at the time of scanning, and their vintage feel provides a connection to the past that goes beyond the mere words of the text.

As bibliophiles, we are always seeking perfection in our work, so please notify us of any errors in this book by emailing us at corrections@windhampress.com. Our team is motivated to correct errors quickly so future customers are better served. Our mission is to raise the bar of quality for reprinted works by a focus on detail and quality over mass production. To peruse our catalog of carefully curated classic works, please visit our online store at www.windhampress.com.

# DEDICATION.

*MOST REV. ARCHBISHOP:*

To whom could I dedicate this book on the life of FATHER JUNIPERO SERRA more appropriately than to Your Grace, who for thirty-four years has held the Episcopal Staff? To-day, the thirtieth of June, 1884, Your Grace celebrates the thirty-fourth anniversary of your Consecration as Bishop. Your Grace was the first to bear the title of Bishop of Monterey. To you then belongs the dedication of these pages, consecrated to the memory of PADRE JUNIPERO SERRA, who planted the Cross at Monterey, and who labored and died but a few miles from it in his Mission of Carmelo. Besides, as Your Grace has been Metropolitan of this Ecclesiastical Province since 1853, it is but just that on that account, without any reference to your many virtues and merits, which of themselves merit the distinction, I should thus dedicate my humble labors. Permit me therefore to offer you these pages as a token of affection and esteem.

Yours in Christ,

J. ADAM.

LOS ANGELES, JUNE 30TH, 1884.

*Most Rev. J. S. Alemany, Archbishop of San Francisco, Cal.*

# PREFACE.

Nowadays it is the common practice to publish the lives not only of saints and heroes, but even of persons of very little or no merit, whose promotion from deserved obscurity is calculated to injure rather than benefit the world. I do not deem it necessary to make any apology for presenting to the public a translation of the life of Padre Junipero Serra, the original of which was written in Spanish by his companion, Father Palou. Though there may be a few copies of this work translated into English, I have been unable to find any. In fact Fr. Serra's life by Palou is so scarce in the mother tongue that the few copies extant are estimated at the highest value. It is true that the principal facts of our hero's life have been published now and again by many California authors, but a full account of his career cannot be found except in the Spanish edition published in Mexico in 1787.

As it is proposed during the current year to celebrate the first centennial of the death of Padre Juniperro Serra, I thought it might not be amiss to contribute my mite in this endeavor to perpetuate the glories of the founder of the Missions of Upper California.

While abler pens than mine are preparing long and elaborate essays on the life and apostolic labors of the humble son of Saint Francis, let the people of California with forebearing generosity pass over the many deficiencies they will find in this translation, and remember only the cordial affection with which it is offered.

† Imprimatur,

FRANCISCUS MORA,
*Episcopes Montereyensis et Angelorum.*

# LIFE OF
# Ven. Father Junipero Serra

## FIRST APOSTLE OF CALIFORNIA.

### CHAPTER I.

Among the saintly sons of the Seraphic St. Francis, there are few more remarkable than the first Apostle and evangelizer of California, the Ven. Fr. Junipero Serra. This holy priest and fervent religious was born on the 24th of November in the year 1713, in the town of Petra, in the Island of Majorca. His parents were Antonio Serro and Margarita Ferrer. From the pious training they gave the young Junipero we may judge they were good christians, who loved and served God. Antonio was a farmer and the worthy couple were noted among the villagers for their industry and uprightness.

Junipero was baptized the very day of his birth and received the names of Michael and Joseph, which names he retained in confirmation. It is a general custom in Spain to confirm children while they are quite young and accordingly Junipero received this sacrament on the 26th of May, 1715, in the parish church where he had been baptized.

At an early age Junipero was well instructed by his parents in the rudiments of the holy Catholic faith; they took care to take him to hear mass at the convent church of St. Bernardino where the Franciscan fathers resided; at the convent he learned among other things, latin and the gregorian chant.

From his attention to his studies, and still more from his piety and docility the parents of Junipero concluded that God had blessed their son with a vocation to the priesthood. To foster his piety they took Junipero to Palma, the Capital of Majorca, and placed him under the charge of a Beneficiary priest of the Cathedral. As time passed on, the ardent wish to be a religious took possession of the soul of Junipero, and faithful to the inspirations of grace he presented himself to the Very Rev. Fr. Anthony Perelló, the Provincial of the Franciscans who, seeing that he was small and delicate, postponed his reception for a time. However, as he was over the canonical age, Junipero received the Franciscan habit, on the 14th of September, 1730, and was admitted, as a novice, into the convent of Jesu, outside the city walls.

During the year of his novitiate, Junipero studied carefully the austere rules of the Franciscans and read the lives of the many saints, which that glorious Order has given to the church; like another Ignatius of Loyola, this reading inflamed his heart with love and zeal for souls; he particularly delighted in the lives of those saintly men who were employed on the missions among pagan and savage nations. On one occasion, with tears in his eyes, he remarked, "During my studies I had a most ardent desire to leave my country and go among the Indians; I took a resolution to that effect." How this desire was fulfilled, we shall see in the following chapter. The year of probation being ended, Fr. Junipero was professed on the 15th of September, 1731. On account of his great devotion to one of the first companions of St. Francis—Friar Juniper—he took that name in holy profession; such was his spiritual joy on that solemn day, that each year he renewed his vows on the anniversary and when occasion offered he would assist at the profession of a novice with pious emotion, saying with fervor: "All good came to me on the blessed day of my holy profession." The good Father continues—"while I was a novice I was so small, that I could not read at the chorister's desk, so I was employed to serve mass. I was sickly during my novitiate, but scarcely had I been professed when I recovered my health and strength and grew to a manly height." After his profession Fr. Junipero was transferred to another convent of the Order, to study philosophy and theology, and he made such rapid progress in these branches that, even before he was ordained, he was made professor of philosophy, and before the end of the philosophical curriculum received the title of Doctor of Divinity. As a teacher he was most successful, and many of his pupils received, later the highest honors in this branch of science. Teaching, however, did not prevent Fr. Junipero excelling as a sacred orator. His sermons were listened to with the greatest attention, even by literary men; his last sermon in Palma was so much appreciated, that a famous orator, not friendly to our Apostle, whispered at the close: "this sermon is worth being printed in letters of gold." The humble Fr. Junipero however, did not seek the applause of men in large cities, his only ambition was to preach the christian doctrine in small towns to a rude peasantry, and still more did he desire to go and bury his brilliant talents amongst the uncivilized children of the forest.

Numerous were the conversions of great sinners, which followed the preaching of the Lenten sermons by Father Junipero.

On one occasion a woman, possessed by the evil spirit, arose in the midst of the audience and said: "shout! shout! as much as you wish, for you will not finish this Lent." The Ven. Serra writing to his friend Father Palou said: "thanks to God I enjoy good health and in spite of the assertion, of the father of lies, to the contrary, I hope to finish well this season of Lent."

## CHAPTER II.

SERRA SOLICITS AND OBTAINS PERMISSION TO GO AMONG PAGAN NATIONS—HIS VOYAGE TO CADIZ—THENCE TO AMERICA.

Whilst Junipero was the object of great applause, both in the pulpit and in the chair of the professor, his desire to labor for the conversion of the pagan nations, made itself more and more strongly felt. However, that he might not take a false step, or be mistaken, he made novenas, and performed other pious exercises, begging God to enlighten him and give him grace to know and do His most holy will, praying at the same time that He would inspire some of his fellow-religious with a like desire. We may well imagine his great joy, when Father Palou, entering the cell of our hero a short time after, told him that he had come to ask his advice, concerning an inspiration which he felt, to labor for the conversion of souls among pagan nations; and asked him what he thought about it. Serra's reply was: "For a long time I have had a similar desire, the only obstacle to its fulfillment being the want of a companion—thank God! the obstacle is now removed! Let us unite in soliciting from the Commissary of the Indies authority to join those missionaries of the "Propaganda" who are destined for America." After some difficulties he obtained the permission he so much desired, and after preaching the Lenton sermons, bade farewell to his hearers, and to his parents, concealing from them, however, his noble project of crossing the

Atlantic to evangelize savage and pagan nations. Then taking leave of his companions, and kissing the feet of all religious, even to the last novice, he, with Fr. Palou, set sail for Malaga on the 13th of April, 1797. It happened that the captain of the vessel was a fanatical and narrow-minded heretic, who soon began to dispute with Fr. Junipero, on religious subjects, so that the poor Father had scarcely time enough to recite his breviary. The captain was a very ignorant man, and consequently very proud, and he would become furious when during the disputations, the Ven. Serra would defeat his fallacious objections against our holy faith. He had for his authority an old protestant bible, and when the good Father quoted texts to refute his assertions, the captain would answer, that the leaf was missing and that he could not find the quotation. One night he carried his rage so far, as to threaten the life of Fr. Junipero, holding a knife to his throat as if he intended to kill him; but, seeing the Father willing to defend his dogmas with his blood, he desisted, throwing himself on his bed to assuage his wrath. Fr. Junipero, fearing, however, that he might again attempt to take his life and that of Fr. Palou, awoke the latter, and both passed the night in watching and praying. Next morning the captain appeared more calm, and during the remainder of the voyage he did not molest them. Fr. Junipero assured his companion, Fr. Palou, that he had never provoked the captain to dispute, but that he thought he was bound, in conscience, to defend the truth of his religion against the heretical assertions of the assailant. On the day upon which the church celebrates the feast of the Patronage of St. Joseph, the vessel arrived safely in the harbor of Malaga. The crew landed, and the Fathers repaired to the Franciscan church, where an hour later, Fr. Junipero could be seen in the choir, with the religious who resided there, reciting complin, and assisting at other devotions of the Order. He, with his companion remained at the convent for five days; then, the vessel being ready, they set sail for Cadiz, where they were to meet the other religious of their Order, who were to cross the Ocean with them. The commissary informed them that five of those appointed, fearing to undertake the perilous journey, had withdrawn, and that there still remained three vacant places. Fr. Junipero then wrote to his convent of Palma, and encouraged by his example, Fr. Verges, Crespi and Vicens joined them. The first part of the expedition set sail from Cadiz on the 28th of August, 1749. It consisted of a president and twenty religious, amongst whom were Frs. Junipero and Palou. The voyage lasted ninety-nine days. The ship was very small, and having on board, besides the twenty-one Franciscans, several Dominicans, and other passengers, the crew was soon put on very scanty rations, and water was given so sparingly, that they had scarcely enough to quench their thirst. Fr. Junipero seemed unmoved, and bore all these trials with great calmness and patience; being asked if he suffered from thirst, he would answer: "not specially, since I have found out the secret of not feeling thirsty, which is, to eat little and talk less, so as not to waste the saliva." Day and night, during the voyage he wore a cross suspended from his neck; he celebrated mass every day, when the sea was not too rough, and employed the nights in hearing confessions. His humility and patience attracted the admiration of all. Towards the middle of October the ship touched Porto-Rico for the purpose of obtaining a supply of water; the crew landed, and it being Saturday evening, the religious repaired to a hermitage, situated near the walls of the city. Whilst going ashore, the superior, being very busy, requested Fr. Junipero to go to the chapel, recite the rosary, and say a few words to those who assisted at that exercise. The devotion finished, the "few words" addressed by the good Father to those present, were the following:—"A mission will be given for the spiritual consolation of the inhabitants of this place, which will last as long as the vessel remains anchored. I invite all to the cathedral to-morrow, at which time it will open." Great was the astonishment of the superior, and of all the religious, at hearing such an announcement, and being asked why he made it, Fr. Junipero answered:— "I understood the superior to direct me to speak thus." The mission was accordingly given, and great and glorious were the results it produced. Such were the fruits obtained by the happy mistake of Father Serra, that we are told there was not one person who did not approach the sacraments, though many had not been to confession for several years. No missionaries had been there, nor mission given in nine years. On the 2nd of November, all being in readiness, they set sail for Vera Cruz, and towards the end of the month, when they were in sight of the harbor, a great storm arose, which exposed them to imminent danger of shipwreck. This storm lasted for two days, and it raged so fiercely during one night that it was universally believed that the end was near and all prepared for death. Fr. Junipero, though surrounded by perils, stood intrepid, and upon being asked if he was not afraid, answered "a little;" but the thought of the noble end he had in view when he embarked, soon dispelled all fear. To increase the danger, during that same stormy night, the sailors became mutinous, wishing to force the captain and pilot to run the vessel ashore, thinking that they might thus be saved. Seeing all human means fail, the religious had recourse to heaven; each one wrote on a slip of paper the name of the saint he intended to invoke, and putting the slips together in one place, drew out the name of Saint Barbara; then all unanimously shouted:—"Long live Santa Barbara!" and the storm abated as if by magic. Two days later, and in favorable weather, they cast anchor in the harbor of Vera Cruz. This occurred on the 7th of December, the vigil of the feast of the Immaculate Conception. Once ashore, they repaired to the church, where a solemn mass of thanksgiving was chanted by the Dominican and Franciscan Fathers, and Junipero was requested to preach on the occasion. He complied, and so well and so graphically did he relate every little incident of the long and perilous voyage, that he astonished his hearers, who formed a high idea of his powers as an orator. The climate of Vera Cruz was so unhealthy, and the weather so warm, that Fr. Palou fell dangerously ill, and measures were taken to transfer the missionaries to the capital of Mexico. Fr. Junipero, asked and obtained permission to make the journey on foot. Without any provision or guide, he, with one companion, as intrepid as himself, undertook to travel in this arduous manner a distance of one hundred leagues, entirely relying upon divine providence, and the hospitality of the inhabitants. God, in whom they placed their trust, did not fail to help them in their necessities. Once, when overtaken by the darkness of night, before they could reach any settlement, and finding themselves near a river without knowing how or where to cross it, they were greatly perplexed; to stay there until daylight would be dangerous; so they had recourse to heaven, and to their celestial guide, the Immaculate Mother of God, and when they had scarcely finished singing a hymn in her honor they thought they saw an object moving on the opposite shore; asking if any one was there, a man answered, telling them to go farther up, and to ford the river at the place he would designate; they did so, and having reached the opposite bank in safety, the man conducted them to his house where they were hospitably received and welcomed. There they spent the night; and the next morning, after having said mass, and before taking leave of their host and guide they asked him what brought him to the bank of the river the previous night; but, receiving no definite answer, they thanked God for His merciful goodness in their behalf, and their benefactor for his kindness and charity, and departed. A few days after, having given to the poor the only loaf of bread they had, a man on horseback, who strongly resembled their first deliverer, gave them a loaf of most delicious bread, which hunger made the more desirable. They then believed that God had sent St. Joseph, or one of His angels, to assist them in their necessities. During this rough and tedious journey, Fr. Junipero received a wound in his leg, from which he never entirely recovered; but, in spite of the fatigue and the wound, they accomplished the journey in such good time, that our Pilgrims were seen on the evening of the last day of the year, 1749, entering the celebrated Sanctuary of our Lady of "Guadalupe," where they spent the night, giving thanks to God and His blessed Mother, for having brought them in safety to their journey's end. Next morning after mass, they directed their steps towards the capital, distant only three miles from the sanctuary.

## CHAPTER III.

FATHER JUNIPERO IS SENT TO THE MISSIONS OF SIERRA GORDA—
THE GREAT ZEAL WITH WHICH HE WORKS—
THE MISSION FLOURISH.

On the first day of the year, 1750, Fr. Junipero crossed the threshold of the Apostolic College of San Fernando. The religious were at the time in the choir, and so edified was he, by their manner of reciting the office, that, turning to his companion he remarked:—"We may consider ourselves well repaid for the fatigues of the journey, since we are to belong to a religious community which recites the divine office so devoutly." One of the first founders of that college embracing Fr. Serra, said:—"Would to God they would send us a forest of such 'Juniperes!'" Fr. Junipero, with great humility, replied: "It cannot be as you wish."

One afternoon, while the Rev. Father Guardian of the college was sitting in the orchard of the convent, surrounded by his religious, he expressed his joy at the arrival of so many missionaries, hoping that some amongst them might be encouraged to go to the conquest of the Indians of Sierra Gorda. Scarcely had he finished speaking, when Fr. Junipero offered himself, saying:— "Behold me Father! send me there," and animated by his example, many others showed their willingness to accompany him on the same mission. The Apostolic college of Santa Cruz of Querataro, was founded principally by Father Linaz for the conversion of the aborigines of Sierra Gorda. This rugged place is situated at a distance of thirty leagues from Querataro, but is over one hundred leagues in extent. Indians of the tribe of, or, nation "Pame" lived amongst its rocks, and though surrounded by christian villages, they were all savages. In 1743 Colonel Escandon was appointed General of that "sierra," and found in its centre many tribes of Indians, though the Augustinians on one side and the Dominicans on the other, had different missions at the foot of the mountains. In 1744, missionaries from San Fernando, were sent to establish five missions amongst them, the principal of which was called Santiago of Xalpan. It was found that there were there 3840 indians. Sickness, and other causes soon obliged the missionaries to retire from the place, but in 1750, Frs. Junipero and Palou, with others were sent to work amongst them. Though saddle-horses had been prepared and sent to them, Fr. Junipero preferred to travel on foot. In consequence he suffered much from the wound in his leg, which became greatly swollen and inflamed, but his courage was undaunted. The Indians who numbered more than a thousand, received the new missionaries with every demonstration of joy. Fr. Serra, began immediately to learn the "Pame" tongue, and then translated the christian doctrine and prayers into their language. In a short time the Indians learned the principal mysteries of the true faith, and how to make their confession in their native tongue. To encourage them to comply with their religious duties Fr. Junipero, like another St. Francis of Sales, went to confession every Sunday, in presence of the whole assembly. In this way, he had in many instances the consolation of seeing over a hundred persons go to holy communion, and numerous were the applicants for baptism. In order to teach the aboriginies to celebrate properly the feasts of our Lord and His blessed Mother, he was accustomed to sing mass, and also to preach to them clearly, explaining the mystery they were celebrating. During Christmas time he would have the youngest of his flock perform a play, wherein was represented the Birth of Christ. In lent, accompanied by his proselytes, he would make the "Stations of the Cross" outside the town, halting at a little chapel built on the top of the hill which they called Calvary. During the devotions Fr. Junipero carried a very heavy cross. In Holy Week he performed all the ceremonies with scrupulous exactness, even to the washing of the feet of twelve poor Indians. On Good Friday he performed the ceremony of the "taking down from the cross," for which purpose he obtained a jointed image of our crucified Lord, and after the "Descent of the Body," he formed a funeral procession to represent the burial of our Lord's Body in the sepulchre. At night another procession was had in honor of our desolate Mother of Sorrows. Then, on Easter day, at a very early hour, he did homage to our risen Lord in a similar manner and also commemorated our Lord's appearance to His Blessed Mother. It is no wonder that aided by so many imposing ceremonies Fr. Junipero gained the hearts of all, and impressed on the rude minds of those simple people the mysteries of the life, death and resurrection of Christ. Crowds came from other villages to Santiago, to be present at the ceremonies of Holy Week, including those of Easter. The good missionary endeavored to excite in their breasts the most ardent devotion to our Lord in the blessed sacrament and to the blessed Virgin Mary, for which purpose he obtained from Mexico an image of the Immaculate Conception, which he caused to be carried in procession every Saturday night, and the participants entered the church intoning the beautiful hymn "Tota pulchra es." Fr. Junipero was far from being a fanatic; he was a zealous Apostle, and while he worked for the spiritual concerns of his children, he did not neglect their temporal wants. He provided the mission with cattle and sheep, and procured seed and grain to raise crops. He expended the three hundred dollars ($300) assigned by the government to each missionary, as well as all the alms received for masses, in procuring seed and provisions. As soon as those in his charge were able to raise crops in greater abundance than necessary for their wants, he taught them to sell the produce of their soil, and to buy in exchange clothes, blankets, animals, tools and household utensils. He instructed even the women and children in the ways of labor, working with them for encouragement and good example. When the Indians were formed in habits of industry, a piece of ground and a yoke of oxen and the necessary implements were assigned to each, and seeing his daily wants so well provided for by means of his labor, this "child of the wilderness" was stimulated to work more earnestly than ever. Then the good Father seeing his charges fond of toil, taught them to build a fine stone church, and after seven years of patient toil this work of their own hands was erected. It was 159 feet long by 33 feet wide, and was adorned with an altar, pictures, and even an organ; a music teacher was then employed who instructed the Indians, and taught them to sing mass. Through the efforts of Fr. Junipero some of the Indians became carpenters, others blacksmiths, others masons and some even painters, the women learned to spin, weave, sew and knit. God blessed in a visible manner all his undertakings; the church was finished and paid for; the granaries were well filled, and the missions were in a most flourishing condition. Just as the good Father was beginning to enjoy the fruit of his labors, he received a letter from his superior, calling him to the conquest of souls among the "Apaches." With a smile on his lip, he bowed his head in token of obedience and prepared to take leave of his dear neophytes, amongst whom he had labored for nine years. As a trophy of his victory over hell, he took with him the principal idol of the place, called in their language "cachum," which means "Mother of the sun." A very old Indian was acting the part of a minister of the devil, in a little temple built on the top of a very high mountain, and to him the credulous Indians would have recourse, that he might intercede with this false divinity for them in their temporal wants. In order to contract marriage, they would present a slip of blank paper to the minister, and then imagined themselves well and lawfully married. Baskets full of these slips of paper, and little idols were found by the missionaries, all of which were burnt, except that already mentioned as being taken by Fr. Junipero, and which was presented by him to his superior, to be kept in the museum of the convent. We are told that at the coming of the missionaries the pagan priest concealed the idol in a cave, and when the soldiers were sent to destroy the temple, (which, though built of the very combustible material, viz.: wood and straw, seemed invulnerable) they were unable to make it burn until the sergeant cried out: —Apply the torch in the name of God and his blessed Mother!" and then the structure took fire and was immediately consumed and a fetid smoke issued from the pile. After the conversion of the Indians, they related these things to Fr. Junipero, and showed him the place where the idol was concealed. When Fr. Serra had departed other missionaries continued to labor with equal zeal for the conversion of the "Pame tribe until 1770, when all being exemplary christians, the college of San Fernando, handed them over to the Arch-bishop Lorenzana, that he might provide for them with his secular clergy, according to the Apostolic bulls of Innocent XI., directing, that when the Indians were sufficiently well instructed and christianized, they should be transferred to the jurisdiction of the ordinary.

## CHAPTER IV.

FATHER JUNIPERO SERRA EXERCISES HIS MINISTRY IN DIFFERENT
PARTS OF MEXICO, BEFORE BEING SENT TO CALIFORNIA.

The College of Santa Cruz of Querataro, had for many years desired to found missions in the war-like Apache nation. In 1758, the government of Spain granted the requisite permission, and the College of Querataro, and that of San Fernando, agreed to found two missions in the open plains of the river San Saba, distant 400 leagues from Mexico. Fr. Alonso Terreros of Quertaro, and Frs. Santa Estevan and Molina of San Fernando, planted the cross near the bank of the stream and about three leagues from the neighboring fort. For the first fifteen days they did not observe any Indians; but soon after there suddenly appeared at least a thousand savages, painted and provided with arrows and fire-arms. The missionaries received them with all attention and kindness, and tried by caresses and other marks of affection to gain their good will. However, the astute Indians were not disposed to be friendly though they pretended otherwise, asking one of the Fathers to go with them to negotiate terms of peace with their countrymen. The Fathers tried to excuse themselves, but in vain; so Fr. Terreros offered to comply with thier demand though he was almost certain they would murder him. Taking leave of his companions, he said:—"Farewell! Soon we shall meet in another world." He had scarcely gone a few yards when he was shot; Fr. Molina seeing he could do nothing in defense of his companion, took refuge in a hut with a soldier, while the other Franciscan, Fr. Santi Estevan, being alone in another hut was barbarously scalped by the savages. The soldier fired at them, but they only became more enraged, and set fire to the hut into which they had retreated; but, on Fr. Molina's throwing into the flames an "Agnus Dei," the fire was extinguished immediately; the Indians, notwithstanding dared to approach but in their attempts to enter the soldier killed several of them. During the conflict a bullet penetrated the arm of the priest, and was not extracted for several years. The valiant soldier though wounded in both legs, continued to fire and defend the missionary till night, when exhausted by fatigue and suffering from the effects of his wounds, and seeing he could no longer maintain a defense, he persuaded the priest to make his escape and to take with him the wife and child of the soldier. The Father feared to make the venture, but placing his confidence in God, and invoking Mary, the "Mother of Sorrows," he passed through a window, and between two camps of Indians without being seen, and after three days arrived at the fort, bleeding and half dead. Soldiers were soon sent to the rescue. but on their arrival they found that the Indians had destroyed all and had abandoned the place. The news of this disaster instead of intimidating the missionaries, only aroused their zeal, and two others were appointed to take the places of those who had been murdered. Of these, Fr. Junipero was one, and though he was aware of the tragic end of his companions, he was preparing to go and face the enemy, when news arrived of the death of the viceroy, and in consequence the expedition was suspended. Fr. Junipero obedient to the voice of his superior, retired to his convent. From this resting place he frequently went to the populous cities of the country, there to preach to and convert sinners, many of whom were perhaps even more degraded than the benighted savages to whose wants he had been ministering. To

follow him everywhere in his labors and travels in behalf
of souls, would occupy more space than the plan of this
work will permit. It will suffice for us to mention the
principal places where he exercised his zeal, from the
time of his recall from Sierra Gorda, to his departure for
lower California, a period of seven years. Twice he gave
missions in the capital of Mexico, and like St. Francis
Solano, he did penance for the sins of its people. Once,
having uncovered his shoulders, he scourged himself so
unmercifully with a chain that the whole congregation
wept and one of those present ascending the steps of the
pulpit, took the chain from his hands, saying:—"I am
the sinner who must do penance, and not the Father, who
is a Saint." And the zealous convert immediately commenced scourging himself so severely that he soon after
died from the effects of the penance. The world may
call the action of this poor man self murder, or suicide,
but if he had a special inspiration from God to do so, he
should be considered a martyr of penance. Besides other
places, Father Junipero, gave missions in the diocese of
Antequera—for eight days he was compelled to sail on the
river Miges, suffering from heat and insects, and incurred
great danger of being devoured by sharks; he was not
allowed to go ashore because the place was infested with
venomous reptiles, and lions and tigers roamed about at
will. After the fatigues and perils of that voyage, he
traveled one hundred leagues on foot. He, with his companions, employed six months of the year in giving missions, passing from place to place, and it is believed that
our Apostle walked two thousand miles in prosecuting his
work throughout the towns and cities of the kingdom.
The remaining six months he spent in his convent, there
recruiting his strength and exercising himself in all the
devotions and spiritual duties of the rigid order of St.
Francis. Many wonderful things are related of Fr. Junipero during this period. Once, after a long journey we
were told, that as the shades of night were fast advancing

and closing in upon them, Fr. Junipero and his companion began to feel some anxiety as to where they would lodge, when, close by the roadside there suddenly appeared a house and calling there, they were welcomed by a venerable old man, his wife and one lovely child. Next morning they departed and continuing their journey, met some muleteers, and being asked by the latter where they had spent the night, the good Fathers answered, "in a house close by." On receiving this reply, the muleteers assured them, there was not a hamlet nor a house to be seen for miles and miles around. Hearing this, our pilgrims believed that their hosts were Jesus, Mary and Joseph. At another time, Fr. Junipero experienced in himself the promise of Christ to his Apostles—Gospel of St. Mark. (10-18.) "They shall take up serpents, and if they shall drink any deadly thing it shall not hurt them." It seems that once during the holy sacrafice of the mass,—at the time of Holy Communion, when consuming the most precious blood, he felt as if a weight of lead had fallen into his stomach, and he was very unwell; however, he drank the wine used for purifying the chalice, but had scarcely swallowed it, when he was seized with a fit and would have fallen to the floor, had not the attendant assisted him. He was carried to the Sacristy, the vestments were removed and he was laid on a bed; all believed that he had been poisoned. A spanish gentleman hearing of the case, came in haste with a very efficacious antidote, but the Ven. Serra refused to take it. Being asked if he would have some sweet oil, he assented, and after having drank it, without effort he uttered the words of St. Mark's gospel quoted above. That very morning he attended the confessional, and the next day he was heard to preach as if nothing had happened. In the convent of San Fernando, already spoken of, there was afterwards seen an oil painting, representing Fr. Junipero with a chalice in his hand, from which a small snake was escaping.

## CHAPTER V.

HE GOES TO CALIFORNIA—WITH FIFTEEN OTHER MISSIONARIES—
HIS WORKS.

The society of Jesus being suppressed in Mexico, in 1767, the Vice-roy, the Marquis of Croix and the Visitor-General Joseph Galvez, agreed to offer the missions of lower California to the Franciscans of San Fernando, Mexico. Though missionaries were then very scarce at the college, the superior found himself bound to accept the trust. The number of Jesuits lately acting within this territory having been sixteen, as many Franciscans were appointed to take their places, although at first the government only asked for twelve religious intending to put four secular priests in the more advanced missions. Fr. Junipero was at this time giving a mission thirty leagues distant from Mexico. Nevertheless, the guardian well knowing his promptitude and obedience, appointed him president of the California missions, and the humble religious repaired immediately to Mexico, to obtain the blessing of his prelate. The Vice-roy having prepared everything necessary for a journey to San Blas, 200 leagues distant, wrote to the Superior-General, and on the 14th of July, 1767, Junipero and his companions took leave of the community, and when the separation took place the guardian with tears in his eyes said:—"Go, dear Fathers, with the blessing of God, and of our Founder St. Francis, to work in the mystic vineyard of California,

which our catholic sovereign has entrusted to us. Go
with confidence, and with the assurance that all will succeed
since you have Fr. Junipero for your superior, and by
these letters I name him president of the California
missions. Obey him, as you would obey me." He could
proceed no farther, for sobs and tears choked his utter-
ance. Fr. Junipero too, was so affected that he could
not speak, and only kissed the hand of his superior.
Crowds were in waiting outside the convent to take leave
of the missionaries. Thirty-nine days passed before the
Fathers reached Tepic—where they were informed that
the Bishop had no priests at his disposal. From this
point Fr. Junipero wrote to his superior, asking for four
other missionaries to complete the sixteen, required to
take the place of the Jesuits. While at Tepic they
learned from the Colonel of the troops who were to accompany them to California, that the packet-boats would
not be ready to sail for some time; so Junipero and his
companions employed themselves in giving missions till
the first day of March, 1768, when they sailed for California. It was in the month of February that the packet-
boat "Concepcion" carried the Jesuit Fathers from
lower California, and this same boat conveyed our missionaries to their destination. The vessel cast anchor in
the roadstead of Loreto on the 1st of April. The day
following being Holy Saturday the religious went ashore,
and during the first three days of Easter week they sang
high mass in thanksgiving to God for having brought them
uninjured to their journey's end. Each missionary went
to the locality assigned him, and in some cases over three
hundred miles were traveled. The Franciscans informed
themselves of the regime observed by the Jesuits, and
then strictly adhered to it. The Visitor-General Galvez
arrived in lower California on the 6th of July, and landed
at the small bay of Cerralvo in the southern part of the
Peninsula, camping at Santa Cruz, three hundred miles
from Loreto. He came not only with the commission to

visit California but also with the royal order to send a maritime expedition to colonize the harbor of Monterey, or at least that of San Diego. Informed of the state of the missions he deemed it best to proceed also by land, and communicated his design to Ven. Junipero, who offered to go in either manner, and to furnish as many missionaries as were thought necessary. Meanwhile Junipero, without loosing a moment visited the nearest missions, and returning to Loreto found the letter of Galvez awaiting him, inviting him to go down to his camp near La Paz, to determine what was best to be done concerning the two expeditions. Although Junipero had already travelled three hundred miles without allowing himself any rest, still he made another journey of six hundred miles to consult the Visitor-General as to the welfare of the missions. These holy men agreed that three missionaries should go with the two packet-boats and two missionaries with the first portion of the land expedition, and afterwards the President should leave with the second division. They resolved to found three missions in upper California; one at San Diego, another at Monterey, and a third between the two places, the latter to be called St. Bonaventura. They began at once to pack up vestments and sacred vessels, and other articles necessary for church uses, as well as tools, utensils for tillage and household goods. Galvez took so much interest in these expeditions that he used to work as a common day-laborer. He helped Frs. Junipero and Parron to prepare for the trip. When writing to Fr. Palou, he said:—"I am a better sacristan than Fr. Junipero, since I packed the articles for my mission of San Bonaventura more quickly than he did for his of San Carlos, so much so that I went to his assistance. He provided the ships, not only with tools, but also with all kinds of orchard and other seeds. He caused the vessels to be duly examined and coated with tar, which he obtained from the Pitayoo. He also ordained, that the expedition should take two hundred head of cattle from the most northern mission of Lower California. This stock under the charge of the mission Fathers, increased with astonishing rapidity. Everything being arranged, the visitor appointed a day for sailors and soldiers to go to confession and Holy Communion. Before sailing, Fr. Junipero blessed the commander's ship and had a mass celebrated in honor of St. Joseph, whom he named patron of the expeditions, and he ordered his priests to sing a mass in honor of St. Joseph, on the 19th of each month to invoke the help and protection of the Holy Patriarch in their undertaking. The ship sailed on the 9th of January, 1769, Fr. Parron being of the party. There were on board the chief commander of the expedition, D. Vicente Vila, a guard of militia 25 in number, with their Lieutenant Pedro Fages; the engineer, Miguel Constanzo, and Pedro Prat, physician of the royal navy, and in addition the officers and crew. They had scarcely left the harbor, when Fr. Junipero started for his mission of Loreto, and on his way stopped at that of St. Francis Xavier for the purpose of visiting his friend Fr. Palou, and presented for the caller's consideration his projects of spiritual conquest. The second ship, called the San Antonio, and also known as El Principe, had anchored at Cape San Lucas. There Galvez went, and having made the necessary repairs, he witnessed its departure on the 15th of February. Frs. Vizcaino and Gomez sailed upon this packet, and before they weighed anchor the Visitor-General exhorted the sailors and soldiers to obey and respect the missionaries. Another ship, the San Jose, was soon after put in readiness for the voyage and set sail on the 16th of June, but was never heard from.

## CHAPTER VI.

#### THE EXPEDITION BY LAND.

Like Jacob, the Visitor-General in his prudence ordained that the land expedition should consist of two divisions, one commanded by Portala; captain of dragoons and Governor of California, and the other by Rivera, captain of the company of Cuera (or leather jacket.)

The latter left the camp of Santa Ana, September, 1768, and upon arriving at our Lady of the Angels, a place then inhabited by natives, Rivera saw that there was no pasture for his flocks, and he therefore advanced eighteen leagues where he found a spot called by the Indians Vellicata.

Fr. Crespi was orderd to join this expedition and upon his arrival everything was in readiness. Besides the captain and twenty-five soldiers, there were in the party a guide whose duty it was among other things, to take observations; three muleteers and a band of neophyte Inians, all well armed with bows an arrows. After a journey of fifty days they arrived at the harbor of San Diego, where they discovered the two packet-boats anchored. Cattle, horses and mules were left at Vellicata, to be attended to by the second division. The Governor and troops went in the van at the request of Fr. Junipero, who remained at Loreto until Easter, to give an opportunity to all the Christian Indians to fulfill their Easter duties. Accompanied only by two soldiers and a servant, he departed from Loreto, stopping again to see his old friend Fr. Palou, who was very much moved at seeing the swollen condition of Fr. Junipero's foot and leg, the more so when he remembered the length of the journey to be taken and the absence of medical skill. Fr. Junipero stayed three days with Fr. Palou, who tried to persuade him to remain permanently and offered to act as his substitute, but Serra replied, "Say no more about this matter, I have placed my trust in God and I hope I will reach, not only San Diego, there to plant the cross, but Monterey as well."

Great was the sorrow of Fr. Palou, at parting with his friend, especially when he saw with what difficulty he mounted or rather was assisted on the mule. Tears rolled down his cheeks when he heard Fr. Serra say, "Farewell till we meet at Monterey," for Palou seemed convinced that they would never meet again in this world.

Junipero went from mission to mission, taking leave of the Padres and giving them instructions, and great was his fatigue when he arrived at Vellicata, where the Governor and others were encamped. As the troops remained there for some time the country was explored, a few huts and a little chapel were built, and Fr. Junipero in concert with the Governor thought it advisable to establish a mission there which would facilitate intercourse with San Diego. On the 14th of May, the Feast of Pentecost, they erected a cross, blessed it and dedicated the chapel to San Fernando, leaving Father Campa for its minister. Father Serra sang the mass and delivered a short sermon on the mystery of the feast. We are told that they had no other lights for that mass but a taper and a small piece of candle, the firing of the musketry taking the place of the organ, and the powder that of the incense. Having to leave so soon, Junipero had not the consolation of seeing any one baptized, but four years after, when the mission was transferred to the Dominican Fathers there were within its jurisdiction two hundred and ninety six christians of different ages. During the three days of Fr. Serra's stay at Vellicata, God consoled him by allowing a few natives to approach him—but let us quote the words of Fr. Junipero, which will show at once the glowing zeal of his heart,—"The day after Easter I experienced a great consolation. Mass having been said, I retired to my hut and in a little while I was informed that some Indians were approaching, I kissed the floor in thanksgiving to Almighty God, since I was about to realize the hopes I had for many years, (to see and speak with the poor Indian) I came out and met twelve of them, all adults except two, who were boys; I saw that what I had read, but which I could scarcely believe was true, that they were as perfectly naked as Adam was in Paradise, before the fall. We talked with them for a long time, and though they saw us dressed they seemed not to blush or feel ashamed of their condition. I laid my hands on the head of every one, and I gave them as many dried figs as they could hold and they began at once to eat the fruit, and with manifestations of the greatest esteem they gave us a net and four fish, which the cook said were not fit to use. Fr. Campa gave them raisins, and the Governor some leaves of tobacco; The soldiers gave them something to eat, and by means of an interpreter, I informed them that a missionary was going to remain amongst them, and then Fr. Meiguel bade them visit him, and tell others not to be afraid and not to steal the cattle, but in their want, to come and ask the Father, who would give them all they needed. They seemed very much pleased, and bowing their heads they retired. The Governor gave Fr. Campa one-fifth of the cattle and some provisions. It was also deemed prudent to leave cattle in the locality for the benefit of the missions which were to be founded, as the result of the expedition could not be foretold. After travelling three leagues Fr. Junipero's foot became so swollen as to indicate mortification; he could not rest a moment, the pain was so intense. The Governor noticing the extent of his suffering, suggested that he should go back; but Junipero would not consent, but expressed the hope, that as Almighty God had brought him so far, He would allow him to reach San Diego. "If not, said he, let His divine will be done." Seeing his determination the Governor ordered a litter to be made, but the humble Junipero would not consent to be carried by human beings, so he prayed to God fervently for help, and calling a mule driver (by name Juan Antonio Coronel) said :

"My son can you find some remedy for my sore foot?"

"What remedy can I have ? replied Coronel. I am not a surgeon, only a mule driver, and can only cure the wounds of my beasts."

" Well son, said the Father, imagine that I am one of those animals, and that this is one of their wounds, (pointing to his swollen limb), apply the same remedy."

The mule driver smiling said: "I will do so Father to please you," and taking some suet, mixed it with herbs, making a kind of poultice or plaster, which was applied according to instructions.

God rewarded the humility of His servant. The patient rested peacably that night, and next morning to the astonishment of those present, he got up early to recite matins and offer up the holy sacrifice of the mass. From here the travelers followed the track taken by the explorers who accompanied Father Wenceslaus Link three years previous, when that divine went in quest of the Colorado river. They continued on this course in a northerly direction for seventy-five miles, to a place called " Cieneguilla," where they turned in a northeasterly direction to avoid the high mountains which had obliged the Jesuit explorers to return without reaching the Rio Colorado. Advancing steadily towards the Pacific they had the pleasure of reaching San Diego on the 1st of

July, after a trip of forty-six days from their last starting point, San Fernando. The soldiers had scarcely discerned at a distance the harbor of San Diego, when they began discharging musketry; those of their associates who had already arrived by sea and land returning the salute. Father Junipero knowing that it had been determined by a council of officers to send back the San Antonio to San Blas, hastened to write to his friend Fr. Palou, from which very interesting letter we quote the following, not being able to give the contents in full:—
"I arrived," says he, "on the first of the month in this beautiful and famous port of San Diego. Fathers Crespi, Vizcaino, Parron, Gomez, and your humble servant are in good health, thanks be to God. The two ships are here, the San Carlos without a crew, all having died of scurvy except the cook and one sailor. The San Antonio, though she sailed a month and a half after the San Carlos, arrived here twenty days ahead of her. The first cause of delay of the San Carlos was the leaky condition of her water casks, which obliged her to touch land in order to obtain a fresh supply. The water so obtained being bad, and not fit for use, caused the sickness of the crew. The second reason for the delay was the mistaken idea, that this port was thirty-three or thirty-four degrees north latitude, when in reality it is only thirty-two degrees and thirty-four minutes; for this reason they went farther north than was necessary, thus prolonging the voyage. The persons aboard growing daily worse from the use of bad water, must have all perished had they not opportunely discovered this port. So feeble were they that they could not lower the boats, and they were in fact nearly helpless. Father Parron labored much in tending the sick, and although thin and fatigued, he is still enjoying good health. I am writing also to the Visitor, College and Commissary Generals, and were it not that Captain Perez is delayed, I could not conveniently complete my correspondence. Neither ourselves nor

the Indian neophytes suffered from hunger or exposure. We all arrived safe and well, thanks be to God. I have written my diary, which I shall send to you at the first opportunity. The country along the route through which we have passed, looks very favorable for establishing missions. The soil is rich and water is abundant around here, and even far back the country is free from brushwood and rocks. However, there are many very high hills, composed of earth. The road for the most part was bad, with now and then an exception to the general rule. For half the distance the valleys and creeks were delightful; they resembled large groves with public walks intervening. In many places vines loaded with grapes, and here and there different varieties of castillian roses can be seen. In a word the soil is fertile, prolific and quite different from that of old California. The longest time we journied in a day was six hours, but the average was four and a half hours. I believe by avoiding obstacles we will be able to go from here to Vellicata in twelve days. The number of natives is very great all along the coast of the southern sea. They subsist chiefly on various kinds of nutricious seeds and by fishing. They make canoes from tule, in which they go out a great way to sea; they are very amiable; all the men and boys go perfectly naked, the female portion are decently clad, even the small babes. They came to meet us as if they had known us all their life time; we offered them food which they refused; all they seemed to care for was clothes, and only for something of this sort would they exchange their fish or whatever else they had. We saw all along the road hares, rabbits, a few deer and many antelopes. The mission has not yet been established, but I will do so immediately after the explorers leave. My friend, I cannot write any more as the captain says he will not wait any longer. All the priests send their best respects to you, wishing you success in your labors. I intended to write to other friends, but it is impossible to do so at present.

From this port, the newly projected Mission of San Diego in Northern California.
July 3d, 1769.

    Your affectionate brother and servant,

                  FR. JUNIPERO SERRA.

The San Antonio, bearer of this letter, left the harbor on the 9th of July, six days after the date of the mission. The voyage lasted many days, and the vessel finally arrived at San Blas, having lost nine of her crew, all of whom were washed overboard. Arrangements were so made that the sick soldiers and sailors would stay at the hospital in San Diego, under the care of Surgeon Prat, and that the San Carlos would remain there anchored until the San Jose reached her destination, when the former, being well equipped, would proceed to Monterey.

It was also settled that the land expedition would leave on the 14th of July, Feast of the Seraphic Doctor St. Bonaventura. The van was composed of Governor Portala with his servant, two priests, Fathers' Crespi and Gomez, two Indian Neophites from old California as attendants. Captain Rivera with twenty-five soldiers, Lieutenant Faxes of the Catalonia volunteers, with seven men, Constanzo, engineer, seven mule drivers, fifteen Indians from old Caifornia as an advance guard, together with others who attended to the mules which carried the provisions. There were in all sixty-six persons. All things being arranged mass was celebrated in honor of St. Joseph and St. Bonaventura, and the party moved along in a north-easterly direction towards the Pacific coast. They left at four o'clock in the afternoon and traveled only seven miles that day. From the diary of Fr. Crespi we will be able to give a more minute account of this first expedition by land, though in doing so we will be compelled to leave for a moment our hero, Junipero Serra.

## CHAPTER VII.

DISCOVERY OF THE HARBOR AND BAY OF SAN FRANCISCO—MINUTE DETAILS OF THE EXPEDITION AND INCIDENTS OF THE VOYAGE.

No matter in what part of California the reader resides he will be much interested in perusing this chapter; his interest will, however, be greatly increased if he happens to live in some of the places discovered and named by these early explorers. From San Diego to their first halting place, those who composed the land expedition, met numbers of hares and rabbits. They stopped at a place where there were several springs, and though the night was well advanced, two Indians appeared on the scene and one of them made a long speech, of which they did not understand one word, and on concluding he presented some sardines to the Governor. In return his Excellency gave him beads and cloth. On the 18th of the same month, (July,) the travelers reached a lovely valley, where the Indians, naked and painted in different colors, came to welcome them. It seems they only painted themselves in times of war and when paying a ceremonious visit. Their chief having made a speech, they all let their arms drop to the ground. They presented some nets of their own make. The women were modestly covered with deer skins. To this place they gave the name of San Juan Capistrano, which name it still retains. On the 24th they perceived the islands of St. Clement and St. Catalina, and they reported San Pedro bay as being five leagues distant. On the 28th, they encamped near a river which they called "Temblores," because all that day and night there were terrific shocks of earthquake. On this spot was afterwards founded the Mission of San Gabriel, twelve miles from Los Angeles. On the 2nd of August they stopped at the spot where the flourishing city of Los Angeles now stands, near a river which they called "Portiuncula." As on that day the Franciscans celebrate the Feast of "our Lady of the Angels," hence, probably the name "Los Angeles." On Sunday the 6th, approaching the head of Santa Barbara channel, they were visited by Indians who by marks on the sand resembling vessels, conveyed the idea that such things had been seen by them. They also made signs to the effect that white men resembling their present visitors and wearing long beards and armor, had at other times come ashore. We read in the account of the expedition of Vizcaino, that towards the close of 1603, he passed with his vessels through the channel of Santa Barbara, which he so named. It was observed that the Indians along that coast had larger tents than common among the natives, and that each family lived in a separate hut. From Santa Barbara the explorers passed through Santa Clara cañon, where there are now so many splendid farm-homes. The dwellings of the then inhabitants were made of a few poles stuck in the ground, forming a semi-circle, brought together in a conical shape, with bundles of sage brush thrown over, leaving an opening at the top which served to permit the escape of smoke and to let in the air and light. Near St. Bonaventura they found the Indians more industrious and athletic, and the women better clad. They cleverly made well shaped canoes of pine, and all their work was well finished. Some of their fishing boats would hold ten men; they would go out to sea some distance, and showed great dexterity in managing very long oars. To work out the timber and stone, they used only tools made of flint, being ignorant of the use of iron and steel. They readily exchanged highly polished wooden plates for a few trinkets. Along the channel the explorers were the recipients of large quantities of excellent fish, which proved one of their chief articles of food during that portion of their journey. The Indians were kind, even staying near the camp all night, playing their flutes but so discordantly that the soldiers had but little rest. After passing "La Gaviota," (sea gull,) on the 20th of August, they reached Point Conception. They passed through the cañon of Los Osos, where San Luis Obispo is now situated, and near Moro Rock. Finding their progress impeded by the Santa Lucia mountains, they were obliged to open a path through the rugged defiles of that range. On the summit of the Sierra even the undaunted spirit of Fr. Crespi began to falter, when he saw that a passage must be forced through a thick forest, and that this must be done with infirm soldiers scarcely able to labor. After descending the Sierra a considerable distance, they encamped near a river, which they mistook for the "Rio Carmelo," but which was the "Nacimiento," the course of which they followed for several days, until they finally, again arrived at the long sought for sea. This stream now bears the name of Salinas.

Fr. Crispi and the commander ascended a sand hill and contemplated the lovely bay of Monterey, recognized Point Pinos and New Year's point, as described by the navigator Cabrera. The soldiers explored Point Pinos on both sides, but did not recognize the port of Monterey, the term of their expedition. Divine providence, doubtless blinded them, that they might proceed farther north and make a more interesting discovery. Here the Governor proposed to go back, but Fr. Crespi and the officers would not consent to it, all saying unanimously, "Let us continue our journey, until we find the harbor of Monterey. If it is God's will, we will die fulfilling our duty to Him and our country." After crossing the Salinas river, they entered the Pajaro valley and encamped near the bank of a stream they called Pajaro, (bird,) because the soldiers saw there a large bird stuffed with hay.

Here they found an encampment of Indians numbering about 500, who having had no intimation of the arrival of strangers in their land became alarmed; some flew to arms, others ran about shouting, whilst the women cried most piteously.

Sergeant Ortega alighting from his horse approached them, assuring them by signs that no injury was intended. He took up several arrows and little flags which the Indians had placed on the ground, at which the Indians gave manifestations of pleasure, clapping their hands as a sign of approbation. On asking for food, the women without delay proceeded to their huts, and soon placed before their guests a plentiful supply of a most palatable paste, which they made from pounded seed.

When the Fathers and company arrived at this spot the next day they found nothing but the smoking ruins of the encampment; the Indians having set fire to and deserted the place during the night.

Where the thriving and beautiful town of Watsonville now stands they saw for the first time redwood trees, which owing to their color they named "Palo Colorado," (redwood.) In this valley they encountered numerous herds of deer, elk, and of another animal which resembled the mule.

On the banks of a small but picturesque lake, probably that where now stands the Catholic Boys' Orphan Asylum, they rested for three days. Meanwhile, the soldiers proceeded northward thirty miles, till they reached the base of a high mountain; but the harbor of Monterey still eluded their search.

Continuing their journey, they, on October 15th crossed over some hills covered with a thick growth of hazel brush and redwood trees. On the 17th they forded a river and encamped on the present site of Santa Cruz; and on the 31st of the same month, they found themselves gazing from one of the sand hills at Point Reys, under which lies the old port of San Francisco.

"Some may doubt it," said Fr. Crespi, "that we have passed the harbor of Monterey, and are in sight of that of San Francisco."

Here their provisions failed, and the travelers were reduced to five tortillas a day. The soldiers went out to hunt, and reported having seen a great inland sea, as far as the eye could reach, (San Francisco bay ) The expedition remained near the bay for sixteen days, and being favored with a cloudless sky, those who composed, were able to form a correct idea of the climate.

On November 19th they passed New Year's Point on their return trip, and on the 21st they encamped at Laguna Creek, near Santa Cruz. Here they killed a great number of wild geese. Towards the end of November they tarried around Monterey, thinking it probable that the harbor was filled with sand; they erected a cross at Carmel bay, at the foot of which they left a written memorandum, intended for the San Jose, in the event of its arrival at that point. Finally on January 24th, after many hardships, and half dead with hunger, they reached San Diego, and found the soldiers there also short of provisions.

## CHAPTER VIII.

FATHER JUNIPERO SERRA ESTABLISHES THE FIRST MISSION IN UPPER CALIFORNIA—WHAT HAPPENED THEN.

Two days after the expedition left in search of the harbor of Monterey, Fr. Junipero with great zeal began to lay the foundation of the first mission in Upper California.

As early as the year 1603, the harbor of San Diego was known by the Spaniards, having been explored at that time by Sebastian Vizcaino.

The 16th of July was most appropriately selected as the day upon which to plant the cross in Upper California, as on that day the church in Spain commemorates the triumph of the cross over the crescent, in the year 1212; besides, that day the catholic church celebrates the feast of our Lady Mount Carmel, whose powerful protection was greatly needed to succeed in planting the faith among the Indians. Father Junipero sang mass, erected a cross, blessed it and performed the usual ceremonies for the establishment of a new mission. Fr. Parron also remained to minister to the spiritual wants of the people. Sickness having prostrated many of them, work proceeded very slowly, and only a few huts were erected, one of which was used as a chapel.

The Indians then began to approach, but as no one could understand them, very little if any progress could be made, except to gain their good will by offering them trinkets and clothes, which they appeared to keenly appreciate. It was observed that they invariably refused to eat anything offered, and if a lump of sugar was put in the mouth of a child, he would spit it out as if it were poison. Had they been as greedy for food as they were for some other articles, the Fathers and soldiers would soon have been in a state of starvation, as their supply of provisions was by no means abundant. The natives were eager to obtain clothing, so much so, that they stole anything that came within their reach, even the sheets from the beds of the sick soldiers. One night some of these thieves were caught on board the vessel cutting the sails and ropes; and in consequence, it became necessary to put on additional guards. In fact, the savages became so insolent and aggressive that the soldiers were sometimes obliged to fire on them to keep them at proper distance.

On the 15th of August, the day on which the church celebrates the Feast of the Assumption of the Blessed Virgin Mary, and when Fr. Junipero had just finished celebrating mass, at which holy communion had been received by some, when the Indians armed with arrows, wooden sabres and clubs, fell upon the missionaries; the corporal with the four soldiers who had remained, gave the alarm and began to fire. Fr. Vizcaino having raised the mat of his hut to see if any one had been killed, was pierced by an arrow in the hand; at the same instant his servant, named Joseph Mary, rushed in, and falling at his feet cried: "Father absolve me, I have been mortally wounded." The Father did so, and in a few moments the soul of Joseph Mary was ranked among the army of martyrs. This death was concealed from the Indians, who in their turn concealed their dead, if they had any. A few days after the wounded were brought to the mission to be cared for by the surgeons.

After this encounter the Indians ceased to molest the Spaniards, and they used to visit the mission without arms. A youth of about fifteen, daily called on the Fathers, and Fr. Junipero bestowed many favors upon him. He also endeavored to teach him a few words in Spanish. After a while Fr. Junipero asked his pupil to entreat some of the Indian parents to have their children baptized ; one day a little child was produced, and from the signs made, the Fathers understood that it was desired that the infant should be baptized. So requesting the corporal to act as god-father, Serra proceeded with the usual ceremonies, but when he raised his hand to pour the regenerating water, the Indian rudely snatched the child and left the Father with the shell in his hand. The soldiers wished to pursue the offender and avenge the gross insult, but Fr. Junipero prevented it, and with tears in his eyes, attributed the frustration of this intended baptism to his own sins. But God, who ever consoles the humble, blessed his labors, and most abundant was the harvest which he reaped. He permitted him to see 1046 Indians, including grown persons and children, baptized in San Diego.

One of the savages who at this time attempted to murder Fr. Junipero, six years after was one of the murderers of Fr. Luis Jayme, for which crime he was made prisoner. Fr. Junipero, in 1776, returning to San Diego visited him, earnestly besought him to become a christian, promising that he would obtain his pardon from the king. But he was deaf to all entreaties, and the next morning, the 15th of August, seven years after he had attempted the life of Fr. Junipero, the unfortunate man was found dead in his cell, having hanged himself.

While Fr. Junipero was laboring under such great disadvantages in San Diego, and on January 24th, 1770, the expedition which had gone north, returned with the news of their fruitless attempt to discover the harbor of Monterey, but reported that they had seen that of San Francisco.

The heart of Junipero throbbed with delight on hearing this, for whilst treating with the Visitor-General Galvez, concerning the first three missions to be established in Upper California, and learning the names to be assigned to each, Fr. Junipero remarked: "And for our Founder St. Francis there is no mission;" to which Galvez replied: "If St. Francis desires a mission, let him show us his harbor and he shall have one. Was it not providential, that the explorers being at Monterey failed to recognize the harbor, and going forty leagues northward encountered at once the bay of St. Francis?"

In view of these facts, what can we conclude, says Palou, other than that St. Francis wished a mission at his harbor. The Visitor-General was of the same opinion; for when the news of the discovery of San Francisco bay reached the city of Mexico, he in concert with the Viceroy labored to establish at once a mission at St. Francis bay. Orders were given to the captain of the packet "San Antonio," that should they reach the harbor of San Francisco before touching at Monterey, and should two of the ten missionaries who were going to California have the courage to remain at the newly found port, they should be supplied with all requisite equipments, including some sailors. The good wishes of Galvez were not however realized till six years after.

Governor Portala seeing that his supply of provisions had run so short, and fearing that with the greatest economy he could not make them last until March, determined if he did not receive supplies from San Blas before March 19th, to abandon the Mission of San Diego. This news, which soon circulated through the camp, deeply wounded the heart of the zealous Junipero, and day and night he solicited from heaven the much needed aid. He formed the heroic resolution, that should all abandon the mission he would remain alone, and wrote to Fr. Palou intimating his high souled resolution.

I will quote a few paragraphs of his letter, bearing date February 10th of that year, 1770. Referring to the expedition in search of Monterey harbor he says: "Those who went returned after much suffering, having been obliged to subsist on mule flesh, and without having found Monterey, judging it to have been filled up with sand; and I am almost inclined to believe the same." One of our great drawbacks, says he, is the want of news and proper intercourse with you; being blessed with good health a tortilla with some herbs from the field, are sufficient for our daily sustenance. On three occasions I have been in danger of losing my life; on the feast of St. Clare and St. Hypolite, August 12th and 13th, and on the feast of the Assumption of our Lady. Fearing that I would be killed, I wrote you a letter of farewell, but as the storm abated I did not send it. If they sent cattle from Vellicatá, forward a little incense, an ordo, and holy oils, in case you have received them from Guadalajara,

My diary, and that of Fr. Crespi, will be copied and sent to you as soon as possible.

On receipt of this letter from his superior, Fr. Palou immediately called on the Lieutenant Governor, and earnestly besought him to order without delay a captain and nineteen soldiers, together with sufficient cattle for San Diego.

The abandonment of that mission was the daily subject of conversation, and so anxious were some that the 19th of March seemed too remote a period. The rumors circulated on this subject were so many pointed arrows in the heart of Fr. Junipero; and particularly so when he remembered that already 166 years had elapsed since the Spaniards had visited that harbor, and that in case it were now abandoned, centuries might pass 'ere they would return.

As the vessels did not arrive in the early part of March, Fr. Junipero went to the captain of the San Carlos and requested, that should the harbor be abandoned by the expedition, he would allow Fr. Crespi and himself to remain on board this vessel to await the arrival of provisions, so that they might be afforded an opportunity to go by sea to Monterey, as he was inclined to believe they had been there, but failed to recognize the place; the captain concurring in his views, consented.

How patiently, yet with what misgivings, he awaited the arrival of the feast of the glorious Patriarch St. Joseph. On that day he sang mass with great fervor and preached; in the evening all was bustle and commotion in the camp, preparing for the departure on the morrow; towards evening the fog which had enshrouded the bay all day vanished; when lo! far away a ship was descried approaching the harbor, but was soon again lost to view; however, this apparition served to encourage all, hope reanimated again every heart; four days later the "San Antonio" entered the harbor bearing joy and gladness to all.

To the powerful intercession of the great St. Joseph, Fr. Junipero attributed the momentary view of the ship on the 19th of March, and he never ceased thanking God for the favor; and for a long time, on the 19th of each month, he had a mass sung in honor of the Holy Patriarch. To the sweet providence God, who never abandons His own, must be ascribed the timely arrival of the "San Antonio" at that trying hour.

When the Viceroy and Visitor-General learned that the expedition by land had left in search of Monterey and the existing need of men and provisions, owing to the non-arrival of the third ship, they determined at once to send the packet-boat "San Antonio" directly to Monterey. The ship set sail under the most favorable auspices; but when within 240 miles of Monterey, their supply of water falling short, they were obliged to take the channel of Santa Barbara, where the Idians kindly lent their aid in filling their barrels. By means of signs they made known to them that the land expedition had gone back; they could even name some of the soldiers. Captain Perez on hearing this was somewhat perplexed, and for a time at a loss as to what course to pursue; finally he deemed it more advisable to adhere to the course assigned by his superiors, rather than that suggested by the Indians; accordingly, he proceeded to Monterey. The loss of an anchor necessitated his return to San Diego, in order to procure one from the "San Carlos." To the unbeliever this fact may seem to be merely accidental, but the good missionaries considered it an act of divine providence to prevent the abandonment of the San Diego mission, and this was accomplished by the momentary glimpse of the vessel the very eve of the mission's abandonment. The immediate effect of which was to enkindle hope in the most despondent hearts. As there was now a good stock of provisions, it was determined to proceed at once in search of Monterey; accordingly two expeditions were organized, one to go by land and the other by water. About the middle of April both set out; Fr. Junipero went by water, on board the "San Antonio," Fr. Crespi and the Governor going over land. Whilst on board the vessel Fr. Junipero wrote again to his companion Fr. Palou, from which I quote the most interesting items:

"Dear Friend: Quite late last night the captain sent word to embark, a summons which was speedily responded to, as I had previously sent on board all necessaries; at an early hour this morning I said mass, since which time the men have been steadily at work, and we now find ourselves at the entrance of the harbor. Fathers Parron and Gomez remain at San Diego; Fr. Juan Crespi and I intend going in the same ship in which the troops arrived. One of us is destined for Monterey, the other for San Buenaventura, which is distant about eighty leagues.

I received no letter by the ship, the reason being that the direction was to Monterey. The death of Clement XIII., and of the election of Ganganeti, one of our religious, are rumors which have reached us. May God preserve the Pontiff. This news has gladdened me in my solitude. A year has elapsed since I received a letter from the college, and nearly the same length of time has passed since your last reached me. At the first opportunity send us some wax and incense, as we need both for the celebration of the Divine Mysteries. Owing to contrary winds, we did not depart yesterday. It is now the second day after Easter, and about seven o'clock in the morning; we are sailing out of the harbor, being towed by a boat from the "San Carlos," which on its return will carry this letter ashore to our Fathers, who will transmit it by a courrier, who will be sent as soon as the expedition leaves.

At sea, before the harbor of San Diego, April 16th, 1770.

FR. JUNIPERO SERRA.

Owing to contrary winds, the voyagers were driven as far south as the 30th degree of latitude, hence they were forty-six days in reaching Monterey. The land expedition made the journey in thirty-six days, having rested on the road only two days.

## CHAPTER IX.

ESTABLISHMENT OF THE MISSION OF SAN CARLOS AT MONTEREY.

It would be impossible to describe the establishment of the Mission of San Carlos in more graphic colors than Fr. Junipero used, when relating the same to his friend Fr. Palou. We will, therefore, quote the letter almost in full, knowing that our readers will enjoy it. It is as follows: "My Dear Friend: On the 31st of May, by favor of God, after a tedious and perilous voyage of a month and a half, the packet-boat 'San Antonio,' commanded by Captain Don Juan Perez, anchored in this horrid bay of Monterey, the same unchanged as it was left by the expedition of Don Sebastian Vizcaino, in the year 1603. It was a great consolation for me to be here, and the pleasure I felt increased with the news received that same night, which was that the land expedition had arrived eight days previously, and with it Fr. Juan Crespi, all in good health. Our joy increased still more when, on the great feast of Pentecost, June 3d, close by the same shore, and under the same oak tree where the Fathers of Vizcaino's expedition had celebrated, we built an altar, and the bell having been rung, and the hymn Veni Creator intoned, we erected and consecrated a large cross, and unfurled the royal standard, after which I sang the first mass which is known to have been sung at this point since 1603. I preached during the mass, and at its conclusion we sang the Salve Regina before a lovely image of our Blessed Lady, which had been placed above the altar; the statue was presented by his Excellency. Our celebration terminated with the singing of the Te Deum; after which the officers took possession of the land in the name of the King of Spain. During the celebration a salute of many cannons was fired from the ship. To God alone be honor and glory. It is not for me to judge why this harbor was not found by the first expedition. It was a year last May since I received a letter from the land of Christians. Let me know the name of the reigning Pope, that I may mention it at the canon of the mass; also if the canonization of Blessed Joseph Cupertino and Serafino Asculi has taken place; if there are any dead for whom we may pray. In a word, let us know whatever could be of interest to poor hermits—sequestered, cut of from the society of men. I earnestly solicit you to send us two more missionaries, who, with the four here, will securely establish the mission of San Buenaventura in the channel of Santa Barbara, the land being better adapted to the purpose than San Diego, Monterey, or any other port yet discovered. I would not wish that for want of missionaries this mission should be retarded. In truth, as long as Fr. Juan and I can stand, we will not be separated; for me it will be the greatest of trials to remain eighty leagues distant from another priest.

Our supply of candles has run out here, as well as in San Diego; nevertheless, to-morrow we are going to celebrate the feast and procession of Corpus Christi, in order to chase away as many little devils as there may be found in this land. Write to the Visitor-General concerning the discovery of this harbor.

Mission of San Carlos of Monterey, June 13th, feast of St. Anthony of Padua, 1770.

Your friend and companion,

FR. JUNIPERO SERRA."

On the very day that the foundation of the Royal Presidio of San Carlos was laid, and possession taken of the harbor, the Mission of San Carlos was also founded. A chapel was built of palisades to serve as church; also apartments for the missionaries in which to transact business; all were protected by paling.

For several days no Indians were to be seen, having no doubt been frightened by the noise of the cannon and guns; but when they approached, Father Junipero at once began to humor them, and by divers ways sought to gain their good will.

The June letter spoken of was received by Fr. Palou on the 2d of August, in All Saints Mission, five hundred and sixty leagues distant from Monterey; the mail-carrier having made the journey in that short time. By the same carrier, a bark bound for San Blas, letters were dispatched to the Viceroy and Visitor-General; however, these dignitaries received the news sooner by the commandant of the expedition, who, leaving the harbor of Monterey on the 9th of July, reached San Blas on the 12th of August.

Lieutenant Fagés remained to guard the Presidio of Monterey, and for want of troops the establishment of the Mission of San Buenaventura was delayed. Fr. Junipero, seeing that the mission could not be actually built at present, began with Fr. Crespi to instruct the Indians, but work progressed slowly, owing to their ignorance of the Indian language. An Indian neophyte from old California helped them, and having learned a few words of their language, the aborigines were made to understand that the Spaniards had come to teach the way to heaven.

On the 26th of December of that year, Fr. Junipero for the first time administered the holy sacrament of Baptism, and the ceremony was often repeated. Father Palou assures us that when he visited Monterey, three years after, he found there 165 Christians, and when Fr. Junipero died, one thousand and fourteen had been regenerated by the saving waters, and of these some preceded the pious Junipero and awaited him in the midst of his Saviour's glory. We cannot deny, says Father Palou, that God, by His wonderful manifestations, helped the missionaries in the conversion of these poor Indians.

Father Crespi, in his diary of the second land expedition to Monterey, relates as follows, under date of May 2d: "After a journey of three leagues, we arrived at one of the salty lagunas of Punta Pinos, where a cross had been erected. Before alighting from our horses, the Governor, a soldier and myself approached the cross, seeking to discover some signs of the expedition which had set out by water, but we found none. The cross was surrounded by arrows, and little rods tipped with feathers, which had been set in the ground by the Indians; suspended from a stick, at one side of the cross, was a string of half-spoiled sardines, a pile of muscles, and a piece of meat. This astonished us not a little; but we failed to comprehend the significance of it; however, as soon as the neophytes were capable of expressing themselves in Spanish, they assured us that the first time they saw the Spaniards, their attention was attracted by a beautiful shining cross, which each one wore on his breast; that when they departed, they left on the shore this large cross, which seemed at night to almost touch the sky, and was surrounded with rays of heavenly light; but in daytime, seeing it in its usual proportions, and, to propitiate it, they had offered it flesh-meat and fish; observing that it partook not of their feast, they presented arrows and feathers, as a token that they were at peace with the holy cross, and with those who had planted it.

This narrative was frequently related by the Indians, and in 1774, when Fr. Junipero returned from Mexico, they repeated it to him without any variation.

The Ven. President wrote an account of this circumstance to the Viceroy, to excite him to a greater zeal for the conversion of the heathen.

The news of the discovery of the harbor of Monterey was received in the city of Mexico with loud acclamations of joy. The Viceroy, the Marquis de la Croix, and the Visitor-General requested the Dean of the Cathedral to have the bells ring forth a merry peal as on festival days; soon the general tolling from the steeples proclaimed the glad tidings. The principal persons, both secular and ecclesiastical, repaired to the palace to congratulate his Excellency on the happy issue. A solemn mass of thanksgiving was celebrated at the cathedral, next day, at which the city officials and dignitaries assisted. An account of this discovery was printed and circulated among the people; copies were also forwarded to Spain, stating that the crown had for two centuries sent vessels to explore the coast of California, or the *South* Sea (the Pacific), and relating minutely the history of the expeditions, by land and by sea, terminating in the discovery of Monterey, and the establishment of the Presidio and Mission of San Carlos, June 3d, 1770. A just tribute of praise was given to the zeal and untiring energy of Fr. Junipero Serra.

Meanwhile, Fr. Junipero visited the whole country, and, with his keen comprehension, saw at once that along the shore was not the proper place to found a mission, the land not being arable; about a league distant, having found a delightful spot in the open plains of Carmelo, he wrote to the Viceroy and Visitor for permission to remove the mission to that fertile spot.

He represented to them the fruitfulness of the land, and the great number of Indians whom they had met in going from Vellicatá to San Francisco. Moreover, he placed before his lordship the necessity of sending missionaries furnished with everything required for the proper administration of the sacraments, and the celebration of the divine sacrifice, as well as agricultural implements, so that the aborigines might be taught to labor and provide for themselves.

He wrote to the same effect to his Superior, and his letter could not have been written at a more opportune time, forty-nine Franciscans having arrived from Spain.

As soon as De la Croix and Galvez received Fr. Junipero's letter, they requested the Father Guardian of the Franciscans to send thirty religious to California, in order that, besides San Diego, San Carlos, and San Buenaventura, other missions might be established under the protection of San Francisco, Santa Clara, San Gabriel, San Antonio, and San Luis Obispo, for which places ten of these religious were destined. Ten more were to be sent to contemplated mission located between Vellicata and San Diego, which were to be named San Joaquin, Santa Ana, San Juan Capistrano, San Pascual, and San Felix. The remaining ten were to be distributed among the missions where there was but one priest. The Guardian readily consented to the request of the Viceroy, who issued the most judicious orders for carrying it into effect. He procured a plentiful supply of sacred vestments, and other essentials for church and vestry. To defray the expense of the missions about to be established, he sent ten thousand dollars, and four hundred for the expense of each missionary. To the Commissary of Marines at San Blas he wrote that the packet-boat "San Carlos" was to be in readiness to transport the missionaries to Loreto, and the ship "San Antonio" would convey the other ten to Monterey.

Reading these things, are we not forced to exclaim: Oh! happy age of faith and heroism, in which the noblest aim of civil and military officials was to promote God's glory and conquer souls! Oh! happy time, when the treasures of the royal exchequer were so bountifully employed in propagating the faith in pagan nations! Have those days gone forever? Ah! how differently are the talents and riches of the nation now employed!

As the vessels were not ready for sea, the missionaries could not set out at once, although the Viceroy was extremely anxious that they should do so. On January 2d, 1771, the ten missionaries bound to Monterey sailed from San Blas, but encountering many storms, they did not reach San Diego till March 12th; here they left a part of their cargo, and again set sail for Monterey on April 10th.

The religious on board the "San Carlos" were not so fortunate. Early in February of 1771, they left for Lower California, but contrary winds carried them as far south as Acapulco; being in need of water, they put into the port of Manzanillo, when they were in imminent danger of shipwreck. The vessel became stranded, but by means of a boat the Fathers disembarked on the unhospitable shores of Colima. The vessel was so much injured that the captain declined to put to sea again; he wrote to this effect to De la Croix, who ordered the missionaries to go by land to Sinaloa, and from thence cross the gulf in a barge. They walked 900 miles, and one of them died of fatigue.

They arrived at Loreto on the 24th of November of the same year. Fr. Palou was then acting as President of the mission of Lower California. As soon as the missionaries arrived, he wrote to the Governor to send troops to aid in establishing the new enterprise; the Governor was unable to comply with his request, consequently the nineteen Missionaries were distributed amongst the missions already established. Meanwhile, the Marquis De la Croix retired from office, and he was succeeded by Bucareli. Galvez also retired, and some time elapsed ere the new Viceroy could well comprehend the current business.

About this time the Dominican Fathers obtained from the King two missions in California. The Viceroy referred them to the Guardian of San Fernando, Fr. Verger, afterwards Bishop of Leon, who, considering Lower California only a narrow strip of land, and not easy to be subdivided, suggested to the Superior of the Dominicans that they take the missions previously in charge of the Jesuits, including that last established—San Fernando of Vellicatá. The proposition having been accepted, was drawn up and signed by both parties, and witnessed by the Viceroy on the 30th of April, 1772. In May of the following year it was effected; the Dominican Fathers took charge of the Mission of Lower California, when Fr. Palou, with nine missionaries, proceeded to Upper California; the other Franciscans returned to their college in San Fernando.

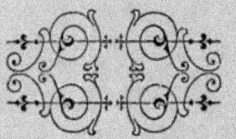

## CHAPTER X.

ARRIVAL OF THE MISSIONARIES—ESTABLISHMENT OF THE MISSION OF SAN ANTONIO—REMOVAL OF THE SAN CARLOS MISSION TO CARMEL.

On the 21st of May the ten missionaries who had embarked at San Diego, arrived safely at Monterey, to the great joy of Fr. Junipero, whose heart overflowed with gladness at seeing the increase of laborers for the Lord's vineyard. As they were approaching the feast of Corpus Christi, he prepared to celebrate it with far greater solemnity than on the previous year. At length the day opened, and from early dawn the Indians poured into the mission. Solemn high mass was sung, a sermon preached and the festival terminated with a procession of the most blessed sacrament, in which the twelve priests took part.

The solemnization being over, in obedience to the order of the Viceroy, Fr. Junipero made the following distribution of the missionaries: Frs. Dumetz and Jaime were to relieve the missionaries at San Diego, who owing to ill health had requested permission to return in the one to Mexico, the other to Lower California, hoping that in a warmer and more congenial climate they might recuperate. Frs. Paterna and Cruzado were destined for San Buenaventura, and Frs. Somera and Cambon to San Gabriel. These having been selected for the missions of southern California, re-embarked on the "San Antonio" July 7th, 1771. Captain (formerly Lieutenant) Fagés accompanied them. Frs. Pieras and Sitjar were selected for San Antonio, and Caveller and Juncosa for San Luis Obispo. Fr. Crespi remained at Monterey with Fr. Junipero.

Priests were needed for the Missions of San Francisco and Santa Clara, and it was expected that the needed assistance would come with the soldiers from Lower California who were expected.

To find a more suitable site for the Mission of San Carlos was Junipero's next undertaking, consequently two days after the sailing of the "San Antonio" he proceeded to the plain and cañon of Carmelo; here he left forty Indians from Lower California, three sailors, and five soldiers, and enjoined them to be expeditious in getting timber and erecting barracks, whilst he would go to establish the Mission of San Antonio. Taking with him the two missionaries, the necessary guard of soldiers and provisions; they traveled southward till they reached a beautiful dell, which on account of its being thickly covered with oak trees, they called "Los Robles." Here they halted, carefully surveyed the place and found a plain skirting the bank of a river; this spot they selected as the most suitable location for the mission, which they named San Antonia. Though in midsummer, they noticed that the river had a plentiful flow of water, hence they concluded that in time the land around could be irrigated.

The place having been selected, Fr. Junipero gave orders to unload the mules, to hang the bell to the branch of a tree, which was no sooner done, than the servant of God seizing the rope began to ring it, shouting as if in a rapture: "Oh Indians come, come, come to the Holy church! come, come to receive the faith of Jesus Christ!"

Fr. Miguel Peiras gazing at him in astonishment, said: "Why do you tire yourself? this is not where the church is to be erected, nor are there any Indians here. It is useless to ring the bell." Ah! let me satisfy the longing of my own heart, replied Junipero, would to God the voice of this bell could resound through the whole world, as Mother Agreda desired. I wish it could be heard by at least all the Indians who inhabit these mountains.

A large cross was made, blessed, venerated and erected; then a hut covered with boughs was made, in which they placed a table destined for the altar, and on the 14th of July Fr. Junipero celebrated the first mass in honor of St. Anthony of Padua, patron of the mission.

When after the gospel he turned to preach, he noticed an Indian present, who had no doubt been attracted thither by the ringing of the bell. At the conclusion of his discourse he said: "I hope through the blessing of God and the intercession of the great St. Anthony, that this mission, at no distant day will be inhabited by many christians, since we see here, what we have not seen in the other missions established, namely: the first fruits of the wilderness. This poor Indian will not fail to communicate to his companions, what he has seen and heard. And so it happened.

No sooner was mass over, than the good Father hastened to the Indian, lavished much attention on him, many presented him with the usual gifts. That same day many other Indians approached the Fathers, and by their gestures made them understand that they had come to live in their midst. They seemed much pleased, for they came again, bringing pine and acorns, which was their ordinary food. The Fathers gave them in return strings of glass beads of various colors.

They immediately commenced building frame huts for the Fathers, soldiers and servants, and a larger building for a church, the whole was protected by a paling. A corporal and six soldiers were stationed here. From the outset the Indians manifested undivided confidence in the missionaries. They brought seeds and requested them to use all they wished and keep the rest for winter. Fr. Junipero remained here about fifteen days and then returned to Monterey.

The missionaries began at once to learn the language of the Indians, and when they had made sufficient progress, they devoted much time to catechising the natives. The seed fell upon good ground; for two years afterwards there were one hundred and fifty eight christians in the mission of San Antonio.

Amongst them there was an old woman, at least one hundred years of age, who came to ask baptism of the Fathers. Being interrogated as to why she desired baptism, she answered, that while young her parents had frequently told her of a man dressed in a habit similar to theirs, who had not come to them walking as other men, but flying, and had preached the same truths they were preaching. The Fathers did not credit the assertion of the old woman till they interrogated other christians, and all assured them it was true; they had heard so from their ancestors, and the coming of the missionaries was a general tradition among them. Father Palou says: "When they related the above to me in my first visit to San Antonio, I recollected a letter which Ven. Mother Agreda wrote in 1631, in which she says that our Ven. Father St. Francis brought to these nations of the north two religious of his order to preach the gospel to them, and that after many conversions they had suffered martyrdom. Having compared the time, I judged that it might be to one of them the new convert had reference."

The Mission of San Antonio is situated in the centre of the Sierra of Santa Lucia, separated from the sea by rugged mountains. Pine trees abound; they bear a nut similar to the pine nut in Spain, of which the Indians are very fond. There are there dense forests of live oak; rabbits and squirrels abound says Fr. Palou, and are as savory as hare. In those early days squirrel may have served for food, now we leave them to themselves or poison them for the protection of our crops. The climate of San Antonio is very warm in summer and cold in winter; frost is very common. A small creek flowing near the mission is frozen every morning until sun rise; thus the crops of corn and wheat are frequently exposed to destruction. It is said that in the year 1780, they had such a frost at Easter, that the wheat crop which had commenced to sprout and blossom, turned as dry as stubble in August. This misfortune led the Fathers to fear the loss of all their grain, and that they would have to recur again to the seed for subsistence. In this emergency they had recourse to the patron of the mission, and St. Anthony did not fail to come to their assistance. A novena in his honor was begun, the crops dried up and withered by the frost were irrigated, and after a few days they noticed that the grain commenced to sprout, and at the end of the novena the field was once more green. They continued to irrigate, and after fifty days the new crop was as far advanced as the dead one had been, and they reaped a far more abundant harvest than that of the preceding year. These facts, says Fr. Palou, and others which we omit, served to confirm these new christians in their faith, and the Mission of San Antonio soon became one of the most flourishing, numbering at the death fo Fr. Junipero Serra one thousand and eighty-eight baptized Indians.

To-day the mission stands alone, the Indians of a century ago have disappeared. Fr. Ambris, who volunteered to bury himself amongst these ruins, ministered for thirty years to the remains of a once populous tribe, and was finally called to his reward. His remains await the resurrection in the mission church he guarded so well. Once or twice a month a priest from San Miguel visits San Antonio.

Fr. Junipero's next desire was to found the Mission of San Luis Obispo, but owing to the non-arrival of troops expected from San Diego, he was forced to postpone it. He therefore concentrated all his attention upon the Mission of San Carlos. He visited the place, and finding the lumber hewn insufficient, he ordered more trees to be felled, and set himself to work. While the other priests remained at Monterey to attend to those at the Presidio and Fr. Crespi was to catechize and instruct the neophytes twice a day.

His dwelling was a poor hut. He erected a large cross which he visited and venerated at an early hour every morning; here too the soldiers would assemble and sing an alabado or hymn; then after matins and prime, Fr. Junipero would offer the holy sacrifice of the mass, at which the soldiers and servants attended with great devotion. Then all commenced to labor, Junipero everywhere directing, often during the day he would cease his labors, venerate the cross, and recite his rosary; this being the only recreation he allowed himself.

The Indians visited him daily, and he delighted them by offering them strings of beads and little trinkets, afterwards he made the sign of the cross on their foreheads, and accustomed them to kiss that holy emblem. He also tried to pick up a few words of their language; he taught them to salute one another by saying: "Amar a Dios," to love God; and this custom became so general that it was adopted even by the Indians, who would thus salute the Spaniards when they met. Scarcely had Fr. Junipero the chapel and other buildings ready, when he called Fr. Crespi and his neophytes to him, towards the close of 1771. They both began to christianize the Indians and continued their labors in the mission till their death. The number of christians at that time being one thousand and fourteen.

## CHAPTER XI.

FOUNDING OF THE MISSION OF SAN GABRIEL—ARRIVAL OF SIX MISSIONARIES AT SAN DIEGO—THE PORT OF SAN FRANCISCO AGAIN VISITED.

We have already seen that the six missionaries destined for the southern part of California had arrived in San Diego on July 14th. Two took the place of the former missionaries who had retired. After the packet-boat left, they began to think of founding the Mission of San Gabriel. Accordingly, on the 6th of August, Frs. Cambon and Somera, accompanied by ten soldiers and muleteers, started northward, following the route of the first expedition. They arrived at the river Temblores, and while searching for a suitable place, they were surrounded by a multitude of Indians, headed by two chiefs, who shouted and threatened. One of the missionaries unfurled before the multitude a banner with an oil painting of our Lady of Sorrows, which the Indians had scarcely seen when, dropping their arrows, the two chiefs came and deposited a string of beads as a sign of peace. They soon called others from the rancherias, and men, women and children came in crowds, carrying seed which they placed at our Lady's feet as an offering, thinking she might eat as we do.

The Indians at San Diego were equally demonstrative in their expressions of joy, when the Fathers presented to their view a picture of our Lady with the Divine Child. Women would flock in from the country around, gaze with rapture upon the beautiful Madonna, and extend their arms as if to fondle and caress the lovely Babe. The unveiling of the sacred picture at San Gabriel produced such wonderful effects on the people that, from that day, they approached the Fathers without fear, and gave evidence of satisfaction at having them in their midst. On the 8th of September the missionaries celebrated their first mass under the shade of some green boughs, and the next day they commenced the erection of a chapel and necessary buildings, the Indians helping to cut the lumber.

While things went on thus prosperously, an event happened which well nigh destroyed this good beginning. It seems that one of the soldiers offended a girl, and the wife of one of the chiefs persuaded her husband to seek revenge. Accordingly, the latter summoned many of his companions, and, while the offender and another soldier were guarding the horses, the Indians fell upon them. However, the parties attacked had time to buckle on their leathern jackets, and place themselves on the defensive. At the first onset the unfortunate chief was shot. The Indians, seeing their leader dead, and finding that their arrows seemed to take no effect, fled in consternation.

A few days later, the commandant arrived from San Diego, bringing with him the two missionaries destined for the establishment of the Mission of San Buenaventura. Fearing an assault from the Indians, he sent the soldier who had occasioned the difficulty to Monterey, to remove him from the immediate pressure of the Indians. The commandant and Fathers were at that time wholly ignorant of the nature of the crime committed. For greater security, sixteen soldiers were stationed at this point. Thus once again was the establishment of the Mission of San Buenaventura unavoidably postponed.

The kindness of the Fathers soon caused the poor Indians to forget the death of their chief, and, strange to say, one of the first children brought to the mission for baptism was the son of their deceased ruler, and the baptismal rites were performed at the request of the bereaved widow. Two years after, the Christians at this mission numbered seventy-three, and when Fr. Junipero died, they had increased to one thousand and nineteen.

The commandant, Fages, next proceeded to Monterey, thence to Carmelo, to visit Fr. Junipero, to whom he related what had happened at San Gabriel. This was a trying hour for the good Junipero, as the foundation of the Mission of San Buenaventura was a project in which his heart was fully enlisted. Moreover, that was the first mission ordered by the Visitor-General Galvez. But the advances made at San Gabriel consoled him, however, and with full confidence in Divine Providence, he awaited a more propitious time for the San Buenaventura enterprise. But his hopes in that regard were not realized until after a delay of thirteen years. In fact, San Buenaventura was the last mission founded by this servant of of God, and he used to say of it, as of the canonization of the Seraphic Doctor: "Tamen quo tardius, eo solemnius"—the later it came the more solemn it was.

Glowing with zeal for the establishment of new missions, Fr. Junipero could not find a moment's rest; accordingly, he proposed to the commandant the founding of San Luis Obispo, but the latter excused himself on the plea of a want of troops; then Fr. Junipero suggested the opportuneness of exploring again the bay of San Francisco, to which proposition the commandant consented. Taking with them Fr. Crespi, they set out in March, 1772. Whilst in the harbor of San Francisco, they learned that the Mission of San Diego was in want of provisions; they hastened to Monterey, and immediately dispatched mules laden with provisions for San Gabriel and San Diego. Fr. Crespi set out also for San Diego, to replace Fr. Dumetz, who had gone to Lower California to solicit the much needed aid. Help was soon sent them by Fr. Palou.

Owing to divers circumstances, the ship which was bearing provisions to Monterey did not arrive till three months after it was due, consequently they, too, began to feel the scarcity of supplies, and they sorely needed that which had been sent to San Diego. Fages, leaving a few soldiers at the Presidio, took with him the remainder, and penetrated a narrow valley called Cañada de los Osos" (Valley of Bears), fifty leagues distant from Monterey, where he killed many of these ferocious animals, and secured from the Indians seed to support his men. In a letter to his dear companion, Fr. Palou, written at Monterey, August 18th, 1772, Fr. Junipero most graphically describes their critical situation. Amongst other things he says: "Thank God, the Fathers are in good health, and the famine which so grievously tormented so many others did not reach us. While waiting for our ship, we received news that two other vessels were coming to this port; one approached within two leagues of the bay, but could not enter. They have whale at San Diego, but here we have nothing. A few mules, tired and half-fed, bring our provisions overland. The vegetables from our garden and the milk from the cows have been the chief support of the people; even these have begun to get scarce. In spite of all, I never regret having founded these missions. Through our labors some souls have gone to heaven from Monterey, San Antonio, and San Diego. There is a great number of Christians to praise God. His holy Name is more frequently on the lips of the people here than on those of many Christians. Some persons fear that from meek lambs they will turn into lions and tigers. God may permit it; but those of Monterey give us reason to expect otherwise, for after three years of experience, we find them greatly improved. The promise made by God to St. Francis, that the people, by merely looking at his children, should be converted to our holy Faith, I now see fully realized; if they are not all Christians, it is because of our want of knowledge of their language.

In San Diego many adults have already received baptism; here we will, with God's help, soon have similar results. The children already begin to speak Spanish.

I purpose going to San Diego with Fagés, about the middle of next September; if your Reverence could come up about that time, what a mutual gratification it would be to embrace after our long separation, and then what a world of writing we would save. Do not come for my sake. Let us both have in view God's glory and the good of souls. Whether with you, or alone, by all means let two religious come up, for the Mission of San Buenaventura or for San Gabriel, to replace those who returned sick. Let those who come be well provided with patience and charity; having these, they will reap a rich and plentiful harvest of souls. During my absence, Fr. Pieras, with one of the priests from San Luis, will attend to this mission. The Mission of San Antonio has very materially assisted us during our time of distress, sending us seeds and pine-nuts. I owe good Fr. Pieras four loads of them. If Frs. Lazuen and Murgia come to this wilderness, let them have patience and courage; no doubt you have need of the same where you are."

At this time Fr. Palou received a letter from the Viceroy, and another from the Father guardian, notifying him of the agreement with the Dominican Fathers, to take charge of the Mission of Lower California. Fr Junipero finding that the ships could not come up to Monterey, and that the mules were not able to bring up the provisions, started for San Diego to confer with the captain of the ship, and on his way founded the Mission of San Luis Obispo. He was accompanied by Fagés; they visited San Antonio and rejoiced to find there so many neophytes. He took with him Fr. Caveller, for the establishment of San Luis Obispo. They traversed the wilderness for about twenty leagues, till they arrived at the Cañada de los Osos, here they found the land arable and a creek with plenty of water. He as usual erected a cross, sang mass and began the mission September 1st, 1772. He left the next day for San Diego. Father Cavaller with two Indians from Lower California and four soldiers with their corporal remained. The only provisions being a few hundred pounds of flour and wheat, and a barrel of brown sugar; the missionary remained, satisfied that God would help them.

After the departure of Junipero, Cavaller set to work with zeal to cut down timber, and soon a neat chapel and apartments for the missionaries made their appearance. The soldiers next erected barracks. In a few days the Indians began coming down from the mountains; they recognized some of the soldiers whom they had met the previous year while hunting bears. They were soon on friendly terms with all, and frequently brought the Fathers venison and seeds; and thus they managed to subsist till provisions were brought. Father Palou visiting the mission the following year, found twelve christians. He left there some christian families from Lower California. He assures us that when Fr. Junipero died there were six hundred and sixteen christians at this mission. Crops were good, and with the products they were able to provide clothing for the Indians. This place is distant from the sea about three leagues, and near the little bay of Buchon; so called by the soldiers of the first expedition, who saw there an Indian chief with a large lump hanging from his neck, called in Spanish, "Buchon." Here the Indians used to fish. It is fifty leagues distant from Monterey, and twenty-five from San Antonio.

Father Palou was of opinion that other missions should be erected between, for, says he, every tribe speaks a different language, and they dislike mixing with each other. Hence, many years after the Mission of San Miguel was built between San Luis and San Antonio, and had numerous neophytes.

Three times was the Mission of San Luis burnt to the ground, and to avoid a similar calamity in the future, one of the Fathers succeeded in making roof tiles, which were used in all the Missions as may be seen at the present day.

The more missions Fr. Junipero founded, the greater was his anxiety to see more erected. San Luis Obispo was the fifth he had established. But his greatest desire was regarding that of San Buenaventura, in the channel of Santa Barbara, where the Indians were very numerous.

With this project in view he started from San Luis Obispo, traversing rapidly the eighty leagues between the latter place and San Gabriel, encountering everywhere great rancherias of Indians. On his arrival he rejoiced exceedingly at finding so many christians, whom he cherished and encouraged to remain faithful to their religion. This was his first visit to San Gabriel. Continuing on his route, he reached San Diego on the 16th of September, and without a moments rest he went to see the captain and commandant of the ships, representing to them the difficulty of sending provisions by land, on account of the distance, and also for want of beasts of burden; there was besides great danger that the Indians might rob the convoy. He urged the necessity of forwarding supplies at once, to prevent the soldiers from deserting and joining the Indians.

The captain alleged as a pretext for refusal that the season was now far advanced, and that he feared to winter away from San Diego; but the servant of God pleaded his cause so well, that finally trusting in the Almighty for a propitious voyage, the officers prepared to sail with the necessary help for the needy missions.

This affair disposed of, Fr. Junipero found himself at San Diego with four missionaries, expecting two others who were coming from Lower California. He now urged upon Commandant Fagés the establishment of San

Buenaventura; but this officer presented so many objections to that and other similar undertakings, that Fr. Junipero suspected that orders had emanated from superior authority prohibiting them; he thought it necessary for one of the missionaries to go Mexico and represent to the new Viceroy the great need of the missions, and to give him correct information regarding the state of affairs. He consulted about the matter with the other Fathers, and after recommending the affair to God in holy prayer, they decided that Fr. Junipero, or some one selected by him, should proceed to Mexico.

The zealous Father, lame and in his sixtieth year, determined to undertake two hundred leagues of land travel besides an intended sea voyage, to secure the interests of his neophytes.

Fr. Junipero embarked on the "San Carlos," which left San Diego October 20th, and after a happy voyage arrived at San Blas, where he heard of the change of missionaries in Lower California.

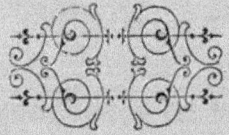

## CHAPTER XII.

JOURNEY OF FATHER JUNIPERO TO THE CAPITOL OF MEXICO—INCIDENTS IN HIS TRAVELS—SUCCESS OBTAINED BY HIS VISIT.

Scarcely had Fr. Junipero set foot on christian soil, his heart still with the Indians, one of whom he brought with him from Monterey, than he turned his steps towards Tepic. On his arrival there he wrote to Fr. Palou concerning some missionaries who desired to go to California. Learning that the Father Guardian had left Fr. Palou free to do as he wished regarding the visit to Upper California, with the spirit of a saint Fr. Junipero said to him: "If your Reverence is determined that there we shall live and die, it will be to me a great consolation; I only say, act according to God's will." Though he earnestly desired that as many missionaries as possible should go from Lower to Upper California, still he says: "If the Guardian should order that only four should go there and the others to return to the college, I have nothing to say, but pray God may apply a remedy to it. Meanwhile let us obey."

God seems to have anticipated the desire of Junipero, as about that time Fr. Palou received a letter from the Father Guardian, permitting him to send seven missionaries to Upper California.

The servant of God proceeded on his journey as far as Guadalajara, where he and his neophyte fell sick of a fever. They were reduced to the last extremity and in the most edifying dispositions received the last sacraments. Father Junipero was not afraid to die, but he feared the death of the Indian boy might possibly retard the conversion of other Indians, as they might suspect that the christians had killed him. However, God granted him and his neophyte a speedy recovery, and they continued their journey to the Capital, where they arrived on the 6th of January all much fatigued, and Fr. Junipero pale and sickly.

The visit of our Ven. President to Mexico was truly opportune, as otherwise the Mission of Upper California might have been abandoned in consequence of the cutting off of supplies by his Excellency, Bucareli.

The Viceroy had in view the abandonment of the harbor of San Blas, from which port the ships sailed annually with provisions for the missions. Heretofore, vessels had departed every year in February, with provisions and necessaries, but this season none had been sent. Some were of opinion that California could be provided from Port Guaymas, crossing the gulf to the Bay of San Luis, a distance of about two hundred leagues, thence overland on mules to Monterey, three hundred leagues more, through a country inhabited by various tribes of Indians. So that according to these wiseacres, provisions before reaching Monterey, would have to pass over eight hundred leagues by land and two hundred by water, being on the way two years, if indeed they would ever reach their destination.

Fr. Junipero having been informed of the erroneous suggestions presented to the Viceroy, and having received the blessing from his prelate, presented himself to his Excellency, and began at once to plead the cause of the poor Indians. The Viceroy received him kindly, and hearing the object of his visit, promised to lend his assistance towards the spiritual conquest of California, and requested him to make a memorial as to his wants. Fr. Junipero promised to do so, but before leaving earnestly solicited him to send some aid from San Blas, since from no other source could assistance be obtained. This first visit produced the desired effect; Bucareli immediately transmitted orders to San Blas, to hasten the completion of the new frigate, and that meanwhile a packet-boat with provisions should be despatched to Monterey.

In accordance with these orders the "San Carlos" set sail, but encountering adverse winds, was driven to Loreto, where it landed its cargo. This delay caused the utmost distress in all the missions of California. Missionaries and soldiers subsisting on milk alone during eight months.

Fr. Junipero in his petition or memorial strenuously urged the necessity of keeping open the port of San Blas, for the welfare of the missionaries; their situation was most graphically portrayed, and the document so well pleased the Viceroy, that he sent the original to the Spanish court; thereupon came a royal order, to the effect that the port of San Blas should remain open, that seven officers of the navy, lieutenants, ensigns, pilots, surgeons and chaplains should be sent from Spain to supply vacancies in Mexico. Having obtained this much, Junipero asked a little more; the extension of spiritual power. His communication was reduced to thirty-two points, wherein were set forth the necessity and utility of these establishments. On presenting it to the Viceroy he said; "In this statement you will find that I say nothing but what is true, and what I consider absolutely necessary to attain that which his Royal Majesty so much desires, viz: the conversion of souls. I trust your Excellency will determine without delay what you deem expedient, since I must return as soon as possible, whether or not I obtain

what I ask; rejoicing if it is granted and resigned to the
"Will of God if refused."

The Viceroy was deeply moved on witnessing so much
zeal, humility and determination, and constituted himself
at once the protector and advocate of the cause. He
called a junta, or council, over which he presided, and in
which all the counsellors voted in favor of the petition
of Junipero.

A plan was drawn up according to law, to serve as a
guide, and to prevent changes in the manner of acting in
the different administrations of the commandants. The
number of troops was increased, presidios or fortresses
were established at San Diego, San Francisco and in the
channel of Santa Barbara. Directions were also given
how to provide troops. The catalonian volunteers were to
retire, and soldiers with leathern jackets were to replace
them, and this change was deemed advisable in the interest of the conquest. It was ordered that each mission
should have six servants, who were to aid in constructing
the buildings and in tilling the land; these were to be
paid during five years from the Royal Exchequer; an
abundant supply of corn, flour, cloth, beans, etc., was given
to the value of over twelve thousand dollars. One hundred
mules were to be distributed among the different missions.
The Viceroy questioned Fr. Junipero as to the expediency of opening a way via the Rio Colorado, by which
they might communicate by land with Sonora, Sinaloa
and other provinces of Mexico, thus preventing future
distress. The Ven. President answered in writing that
he considered it very expedient, especially if by doing so
they could communicate with New Mexico, until they
would be able to find a route to Monterey.

As soon as the Viceroy saw his plan approved, he
issued orders to Captain Anza to go from the Presidio de
Tibac on the frontiers of Sonora to that of Monterey,
through the rivers Gila and Colorado. The captain hap-

pily executed these orders. The heart of the Viceroy was so inflamed by the long, earnest conversations which he held with the zealous servant of God, that no thought now occupied him other than the extension of these missions as far north as possible. He proposed to the Father to send a maritime expedition farther north. Junipero had nothing more at heart than this, and he encouraged the plan by suggesting that the new frigate commanded by Perez, might after leaving Monterey explore the coast, in which suggestion the Viceroy concurred.

Our Apostle having obtained far more than he expected, was impatient to return to his adopted children. With the blessing of his Father Guardian, and after kissing the feet of all the Fathers he bade them farewell forever. Tears came to the eyes of many when considering the feebleness and old age of their companion, but none would dare prevent his going. Believing that he would die on the road, he wished to take the shortest route possible to his dear Monterey. Accordingly in September, 1773, he set out, accompanied by Father Pablo Mugartegui and his dear neophyte. After a journey of about two hundred leagues he reached Tepic. Here finding that the ships were not ready, he was obliged to wait till January. Meantime he gave orders that the provisions for the northern missions should be stored in the frigate destined for Monterey, and that those intended for the other missions should be carried by the packet-boat "San Antonio."

Fr. Junipero finally sailed from Tepic on January 24th, 1774, in the frigate "Santiago la nueva Galicia."

As he embarked, some one remarked to him; "Father, your prophecy made when passing here is now fulfilled. After we had received orders to suspend all work on the frigate, you said to us, 'hurry up and finish the vessel, for in it I shall return to Monterey.' We laughed at you then, as our orders were to destroy what had been done and save the iron." Junipero answered mildly: "the great desire I entertained of seeing a large vessel, capable of bringing abundance of bread to my poor children, caused me to speak in that way. Let us be grateful to God that my wishes have been granted." And after thanking those who had labored in the construction of the ship he bade them farewell.

Though destined for Monterey, Junipero incidentally touched at San Diego after a voyage of forty-nine days. His sole desire was to be at once with his beloved neophytes at Monterey; however, he rejoiced at seeing the new christians of San Diego; and while there he resolved to continue the journey on foot, and visit all the missions, bringing with him the provisions which were sorely needed every where. He carried this resolution into effect, and on his route he met Captain Don Juan Bautista Anza, who was returning from Monterey to report to the Viceroy that communication was open between the province of Sonora and California. From him he learned of the distress in Monterey, at which place the people were forced to subsist on herbs and milk. With a sad heart Junipero hastened to their succor; but he found on arriving that the frigate, laden with provisions, was three days ahead of him, having made its appearance on the 9th of May. It is needless to say that universal joy prevailed when it was understood that the danger of famine had vanished, and that the beloved Father was once more in the midst of his flock.

## CHAPTER XIII.

EXPLORATION BY SEA TO THE NORTH OF MONTEREY.

To satisfy the noble desires of his Excellency the Viceroy, the frigate "Santiago" was sent to explore the coast as far north as practicable, and to ascertain whether the country was inhabited by roaming tribes of Indians. Mindful of the promise made by God to St. Francis, that the mere sight of his religious will tend to convert the Indians, the Viceroy desired that one or two missionaries should go on board. Frs. Crespi and Peña were selected for this expedition, and, full of confidence in God, they sailed from Monterey on the 11th of June, 1774.

They passed as far north as the 55° degree, British Columbia, where they noticed an island which they called Santa Margarita, owing to the fact that it was discovered on the feast of that saint. Whilst surveying the coast, it was observed that the island was well peopled by Indians. Several attempts were made to land for the purpose of planting the holy cross, but contrary winds prevented. However, the voyagers had some communication with the Indians, as the latter approached in their canoes, and some even boarded the frigate and exchanged well polished woods, hair blankets, and mats made from the bark of trees, with the sailors for pieces of iron and bead trinkets. We are told that these Indians were of uniform height, dressed in skins and hair-cloth, and were amiable in disposition; their women decently covered and of fine appearance, but disfigured by wearing a wooden tablet in the lower lip, fastened by means of a perforation. The effect of this peculiar ornamentation was to drag down and distort the mouth.

This expedition returned on the 27th of August of the same year. Reports were sent to the Viceroy, who, not being satisfied, ordered another cruise, directing that it should proceed still farther north, and search for a good harbor where the cross and the Spanish flag could be raised.

The second expedition, consisting of the frigate "Santiago" and a schooner, both under command of Don Bruno Ezeta, sailed from San Blas about the middle of March, 1775. Frs. Miguel Campo and Benito Sierra accompanied it. After contrary winds, which brought them as far south as the 17° degree, it became more favorable, and they sailed north to the 41°; here they touched land, and found a moderately good harbor; they took possession of the place, elevated a cross and the Spanish standard; here, too, they sang mass and preached. It being the feast of the Most Holy Trinity, the place was called and is now known as Trinity Bay. On the 13th of July, they touched upon a lovely spot in latitude 47° 23'. Here, again, they anchored and erected a cross. On the 30th of the same month, the schooner was separated from the frigate, and they did not meet again till October, at the harbor of Monterey.

The frigate went as far north as the $47\frac{1}{2}$ degree; but the captain, finding the scurvy had broken out among the crew, determined to return, to survey the coast and search for the schooner, and he ultimately arrived at Monterey, August 29th of that year.

The schooner had followed the coast in search, also, of the frigate, and went as far north as the 58th degree, where a good harbor was discovered, which they called

Our Lady of Remedios; they took possession of it, and erected a cross. An attempt was made to advance farther north; but a strong gale forced them back to the 55th degree; here they found a strait, which they supposed to be the celebrated Paso del Norte, or Northern Passage, so much sought for by the English. In honor of the Viceroy who sent them, they called it Bucareli. They surveyed and made maps of the coast. On the 3d of October, they reached Punta Reyes, where they discovered a good harbor. Here more than two hundred Indians greeted them, and that night signalized the occasion by making a large fire. On the following day the party was in imminent danger of shipwreck, owing to the roughness of the sea. They lost a boat, and fearing that the vessel might also go down, they weighed anchor, named the place Bodega, in honor of the captain of the schooner, and sailed for Monterey, which they reached on the 7th of October. Here, to their great surprise, they found the frigate and the packet-boat "San Carlos." Eight days later, they all went to the Mission of San Carlos, where a mass of thanksgiving was celebrated in honor of Our Lady, during which every one, from the highest officer to the humblest sailor, received the Holy Communion.

The reader may think that, in relating the account of these explorations to the north, we digress too much from our principal subject, namely: The Life and Apostolic Labors of Fr. Junipero. But this view, if taken, would be mistaken, for the digression was necessary; in fact, it was a happy one, since it redounded to the honor and glory of our hero, as may be seen by the letter which the Viceroy, Bucareli, wrote, thanking him for the prosperous issue of the explorations.

The new discoveries, made by the ships of the King, says the Viceroy, are the object of your letter, in which you send me congratulations, which I received with pleasure; but your Reverence is deserving, also, of many thanks for having celebrated such an event with all possible solemnity. I am satisfied that your zeal and that of the other Fathers will be the best guarantee for the extension of the gospel, to which end are directed all the pious wishes of our monarch. This letter is dated Mexico, January 20th, 1776.

Nor was the zeal of Bucareli diminished. He sent another expedition in the year 1779, the incidents of which will be narrated in order to enable us to more intelligently proceed with the life of Fr. Junipero. Bucareli sent to Peru for a new frigate, called "Favorita," which, with the "Princesa," he fitted for a third exploration, obtaining at the time from the College of San Fernando, in Mexico, two missionaries, Frs. Riobo and Noriega, to accompany the venture. They sailed from San Blas, February 12th, 1779. It was agreed that, should they separate, a meeting would be had at the 55th degree north—*i. e.*, at the Strait of Bucareli—which they reached safely on the 3d of May. They found here an inland sea and a cluster of islands, located in what is called at present British Columbia. They held communication with many tribes of Indians, whom they describe as robust and well formed. They bought from these natives three boys and three girls, whom they afterwards instructed and baptized. They named this harbor Bucareli, in honor of the Viceroy. On the 1st of August they found themselves as far north as the 60th degree, the coast tending in a northwesterly direction. There, we are told, was discovered an extensive port, well protected from the wind by an abundance of trees. They landed, and called the harbor Santiago. It is supposed that this was Cook's Inlet. The navigators landed, and on the summit of a hill, close by, they formed a procession, and, carrying the cross, sang the hymn "Vexilla Regis."

A pilot and some troops were sent to examine the harbor and ascertain its extent. After advancing for some distance, they encountered two canoes with peaceable Indians, and returned without further adventure. Meanwhile, those on board the frigate had frequent and easy intercourse with the natives. They noticed among the Indians who visited them a man who manifested not the least surprise at sight of the frigate, and who, by signs, made them understand that at a little distance there were many large ships, which led his hearers to suppose that the Russian settlement was not far off; they even suspected that the man was a Russian under the guise of an Indian, and had been sent to watch the movements of the Spanish. They were confirmed in this opinion by the fact that there arose before them the volcano then called by the Russians St. Elias.

When the surveying detachment returned, all supposed that the frigates would proceed to examine the newly found arm of the sea; but contrary orders were given, namely: To investigate only along the coast. As they were then about 59 degrees north latitude, they were in imminent danger from a heavy fog, accompanied with rain, which lasted for twenty-five hours, and in consequence of which they found it impossible to ascertain their whereabouts.

Then the commandant ordered that the image of Our Lady, under the title of "Regla," should be brought on deck, and a Salve Regina was sung in her honor. The fog thereupon totally disappeared, and the adventurers saw before them a beautiful and capacious bay, in which, after anchoring, they called Our Lady of Regla.

The season being now far advanced, and many of the men sick, the commandant declared the explorations at an end, and gave orders to sail promptly for one of the ports of California. This order was complied with, and the vessels in question entered the Bay of San Francisco on the 14th and 15th of September; here they remained till October. A feast of thanksgiving celebrated the deliverance of the expedition from so many perils. Mass was sung and a sermon preached on October 3d. The next day, being the feast of St. Francis, patron of that mission, another mass was solemnized, and another procession took place, in honor of the Saint. Fr. Palou was then located at and in charge of that mission.

There he had the pleasure of baptizing the three boys brought from the north, leaving a fourth, who was a little older, for further instruction. Whilst preparing to leave this port, news came that Bucareli, the Viceroy, had died. This news gave rise to universal sorrow, as the deceased had proved himself a great benefactor of the missions. Father Palou, with a true Christian spirit, expressed the hope that his soul had already received its merited reward.

It is true that Fr. Junipero did not work personally in these expeditions, and it may seem that we might have omitted the details given concerning them. Still, it will always be to the honor of Serra that his visit to Mexico awakened a desire in the heart of his Excellency, the Viceroy, to encourage the making of discoveries, and that this was accomplished by that missionary's wise and forcible suggestions. "The port of Trinity," says Bucareli, in a letter to Fr. Junipero, "discovered by Bruno Ezeta, invites us to a settlement to which your zeal shall contribute."

Had the life of the zealous Viceroy been prolonged, and had he learned the result of the last expeditions, and witnessed the effect of Fr. Junipero's arrival—*i. e.*, the great prosperity and productiveness of the missions—he would no doubt have extended the missionary establishments as far north as the famous port called in his honor Bucareli.

According to Fr. Palou, the increase of cattle was truly wonderful. Only eighteen head were given to each mission when founded; but, in 1784, the returns show that the nine missions then existing had 5,384 head of cattle, 5,269 head of sheep, and 4,294 goats. The crops of wheat, corn, barley, beans, and other cereals, amounted to 15,800 bushels, which not only furnished enough to provide for the neophytes, but the soldiers were permitted to purchase adequate supplies from the same source.

Fr. Palou concludes his narrative of these maritime expeditions by telling us that the first fruits of missionary exertion among the northern Indians, viz., the youths brought and baptized in San Francisco, had gone to heaven, where they will, says that pious man, intercede for the conversion of their nation. The sons of St. Francis had never before advanced so far north, and even afterwards the missionary establishments were not pushed greatly beyond the locality where Palou wrote his history.

Other missionaries, in due course of events, continued the good work, and the Catholic Church extends now as far north as Alaska, knowing no other barrier than that of the frozen sea.

## CHAPTER XIV.

APOSTOLIC LABORS OF FATHER JUNIPERO SERRA AFTER HIS RETURN FROM MEXICO—FATHER JAYME IS PUT TO DEATH IN HIS MISSION OF SAN DIEGO.

The Ven. President arrived at his Mission of San Carlos about the middle of May, 1774, and after a few days spent in unloading the provisions and in hastening the expedition to the north, as related in the last chapter, he directed all his energies to the instruction of his neophytes, to prepare them for baptism; day after day he was surrounded by them, and soon the number of baptized was very great.

About this time there arrived at the Presidio Captain Rivera, who came to replace Captain Fagés of the catalonian volunteers, it having been decided by the the council of war that the troops wearing the leathern jackets were better adopted for these places.

Our Apostle, though well aware that the number of christians in each mission was increasing, was not satisfied; he desired the establishment of other similar institutions; but the new regulations forbade this until there should be sufficient troops; unless, said the code, a few soldiers can be taken from the missions already established, and by this means the requisite number obtained for additional establishments. Fr. Junipero consulted with Captain Rivera on the subject. That officer agreed that a new mission should be built and he allotted six soldiers for that purpose. The proposition was referred to the Viceroy, who in a letter of August 17th, approved the establishment of a new mission between San Diego and San Gabriel, to be called San Juan Capistrano.

Frs. Lazuen and Amurrio were appointed for the new mission; they left Monterey accompanied by a few soldiers, with the necessary articles. Fr. Amurrio remained at San Gabriel, while Fr. Lazuen with the Lieutenant Commander of the Presidio went in search of a suitable location for the mission. Towards the end of October they left San Diego, and having found a desirable spot they erected a cross and made a hut of the boughs of trees, and in that Fr. Lazuen celebrated the holy mass for the first time. This was on October 30th, the Octave of the Patron Saint, St. Juan Capistrano. The Indians showed that they were friendly, and even assisted the new comers to cut timber. Eight days afterwards Fr. Amurrio arrived with provisions, and all hearts rejoiced at the bright prospects. That very same evening a messenger arrived from San Diego, with the sad news that the Indians had revolted, set fire to the buildings, and killed one of the missionaries, Fr. Jayme. The lieutenant and sergeant, taking with them some soldies, started in haste for San Diego, begging the Fathers to do the same, who hastily buried the bells, and taking all their cargo, left also for the scene of the disaster.

In November 1775, Fr. Luis Jayme and his companion Fr. Vincent Fuster were busily engaged in instructing the neophytes. They had reaped an abundant harvest, so great indeed, that on the 3rd of October, 1775, they baptized sixty Indians. This kindled the jealousy of the enemy of souls, at whose instigation the Indians attempted the destruction of the mission. The previous year the Fathers had moved to a very fertile spot, about two leagues distant from the harbor of San Diego, and from the Presidio. This move emboldened the savages to make the attack about to be described. Two of the recently baptized neophytes, under pretence of visiting some relatives, left the mission, and went from rancheria to rancheria, telling the natives that the Fathers were about to baptize them by force, stating the number who had been made christians in one day. Some credited the story, others doubted it; but the majority yielded to the persuasions of the two apostates, who left no means untried to arouse indignation against the priests. Meanwhile all went on as usual at San Diego, nothing indicated the heineous crime about to be perpetrated. The Indians were quiet, the traitorous pair having been missed, search was made for them by the soldiers, and information was received that the fugitives had gone to the mountains. Over a thousand Indians assembled, mostly strangers to each other; they had been convened by crafty ringleaders and were well armed with arrows and "macanas," which latter is a wooden sword used by the Indians, and is in form like a cimitar. They were to divide themselves into two parties, one to attack the mission, the other the presidio; this latter attack was to be made after the mission buildings had been set on fire.

On the night of the 4th of November, the hostiles arrived in the valley of the San Diego river, where dividing according to understanding, one party proceeded to the presidio, the other fell upon the mission, taking the precaution to place centries in all the huts of christian Indians, threatening the latter with death if they dared to move or give the alarm. The greater number of the assailants rushed to the church and vestry, which they robbed of its sacred vessels and vestments. They next advanced upon the barracks, and finding the soldiers asleep, snatched fire brands from the hearth and set fire to the barracks and adjacent buildings. The blaze and the horrid shouts of the miscreants awoke both Fathers and soldiers; when the latter seized their arms for defense, the Indians had already commenced to discharge their arrows. Fr. Vincent seeing danger, took the son and nephew of the officer of the Presidio, and fled hastily to where the soldiers were standing. In one building lived the blacksmith and the carpenter of the mission, with them resided Ursulino the carpenter of the Presidio, who having become sick, had been brought to the mission to recuperate. Fr. Jayme who slept in another building, seeing the conflagration judged it to be accidental. He rushed out, and meeting a large group of Indians greeted them with the usual salutation: " Let us love God my children." When the Indians caught sight of the Father, they charged upon him with wolf like ferocity, and dragged him to the creek, and after stripping him of his habits they beat him, and otherwise ill treated him until he fell dead, his body pierced with numerous arrows; nor were the murderous wretches satiated, they crushed the holy man's head and mutilated his body till his hands only were recognizable, those were left untouched. It would seem that divine providence preserved his consecrated hands as a proof of his innocence, and to proclaim that they had ever been employed in doing good. Meanwhile another band of Indians assailed the hut in which were the carpenter and blacksmith, the latter came forth with drawn sword, but immediately fell dead, pierced by an arrow; the carpenter seized and discharged the deceased's gun, killing a savage. The other enemy retreated, allowing the carpenter an opportunity to join the soldiers. Poor Ursulino being unable to move, received a mortal arrow wound. Aware of his situation, he cried out, "Oh, Indian thou hast killed me! may God forgive thee." When the Indians learned that one of the Fathers had been assassinated, they eagerly inquired which of the two, and on being told it was the "rezador," (the one who was always praying) they gave vent to their joy by wild shouting.

The band intrusted for the destruction of the presidio, fearing discovery, returned and joining those at the mission, all now fell on the barracks. The soldiers defended themselves valiantly, especially the corporal, who performed heroic deeds of valor. Seeing the terrible effects of the gun, the savages set fire to the building, and the roof being of straw and the walls of paling, the inmates were soon obliged to abandon it. They sought refuge in a little room of adobe which had served as a kitchen; this had but three walls, a roof of dry branches, and the remaining side was wholly exposed to the enemy; the soldiers ran to the burning building to procure bundles and boxes with which to shelter themselves. In doing this two soldiers were wounded and rendered unable to defend themselves further. There now remained only the corporal and one soldier and the carpenter to face the enemy. The corporal being a sharp-shooter, told the others to load the guns and that he would do the shooting; in consequence any Indian who approached this place was killed or wounded. The infuriated savages seeing that the adobe walls protected their foes from the arrows, burned the dry branches with which the room was covered, but as the inflamable material was scarce, the fire did not oblige the soldiers to leave. However, there was great danger that the powder upon which the Spaniards relied, would explode. Fr. Vincent seeing the character of the peril covered the powder with his habit, and in doing so endangered his own life.

The Indians perceiving that the fire did not oblige their proposed victims to surrender, threw burning coals and pieces of adobe over the walls, and they succeeded in wounding the Father, but not seriously. Our gallant little party defended themselves bravely till day break, when the Indians fearing that help would come from the Presidio, fled, carrying with them the wounded and the dead.

Scarcely had they retired when the christian Indians came out from their huts, and with many tears and lamentations related the story of their confinement, and their inability to render assistance during the trials of that night. The Father anxiously inquired for his missing companion, Fr. Jayme. Search was immediately made for him and his mutilated remains were discovered near the creek where the massacre took place. His body was tenderly raised with the greatest reverence, and was born to Fr. Vincent, who hearing the lamentations of the mourners, comprehended at once the nature of the bereavement. At the sight of the mangled body of his beloved companion the good priest almost lost consciousness.

He had two biers made on which the bodies of Fr. Jayme and that of the blacksmith were borne to the chapel of the Presidio, where they were interred. The carpenter Ursulino died five days after this date, having in a truly christian spirit bequeathed his savings to his murderers. Soon soldiers arrived from the projected Mission of San Juan Capistrano; here they awaited orders from their President, Fr. Junipero Serra.

The news of the disastrous events at San Diego reached Monterey on the 13th of December, and, though late at night, Captain Rivera set out at once for the Mission of of San Carlos, to communicate the sad tidings to Fr. Junipero; who on hearing of the death of Fr. Jayme, exclaimed: "Thanks be to God that land is watered; now we will obtain the conversion of the Indians of San Diego." The next day a requiem mass was sung, at which six priests assisted, among them Fr. Palou, who affirms that the zeal and virtues of the murdered priest were so great, that in the opinion of all his soul needed not their supplications, but they piously believed that he had gone directly to heaven to receive a martyr's crown. However, the President adoring the judgments of God, which are inscrutable, determined that each priest should celebrate twenty masses for him, and an understanding to that effect was accordingly made.

Fr. Junipero wrote so his Guardian and the Viceroy, sorely lamenting the rash act of the poor Indians, and fearing it might retard their conversion. Like a true Father he pleaded with his Excellency for the misguided natives, and implored his clemency for them. At the same time he begged that the number of troops should be increased, so that the foundation of the contemplated missions should not be retarded.

Captain Rivera left Monterey December 16th, and visited the Missions of San Antonio and San Luis Obispo, which he found prosperous and peaceful. At San Gabriel he met Captain Anza, who with forty soldiers had come from Sonora, and he also brought some people to settle the Port of San Francisco. Both captains agreed to go down to San Diego to search for and punish the ringleaders of the revolt. They at once wrote to the Viceroy to that effect. His Excellency received the letters of these officers, but that of Fr. Junipero miscarried. Thinking the communication had been mislaid or delayed, he wrote to the Ven. President a letter of condolence, at the same time informing him of the precautions he had taken to prevent a similar disaster, and of the strict orders he had issued to the newly appointed Governor of California, Don Felipe Neve, who was then setting out with twenty-five more soldiers, and was also providing for other recruits. Eight days after he had written this letter, which was dated Mexico, March 26th, 1776, he received Fr. Junipero's missive to which he replied: "In view of the prudent and christian reflections expressed in your letter, inclining rather to soften the rebels by kindness than to punish them; I have written to the Commander Rivera so to act, thinking it the best method of pacifying and winning them, and such a policy would perhaps also aid us in gaining the neighboring tribes, who seeing that they are treated with lenity, while on account of their excesses they deserve punishment. I have given orders to my officers to rebuild the Mission of San Diego, and to establish that of San Juan Capistrano." This letter bears date April 3rd, 1776.

Had Fr. Junipero received this news in due time, he would have been spared much anxiety and suffering regarding the rebuilding of San Diego and the establishment of San Juan Capistrano.

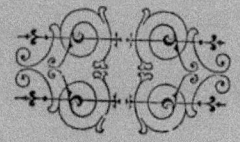

## CHAPTER XV.

FATHER JUNIPERO GOES TO SAN DIEGO—USELESS EFFORTS TO RE-ESTABLISH THE MISSION—ARRIVAL OF TROOPS—THE MISSION IS RE-ESTABLISHED, AND THAT OF SAN JUAN CAPISTRANO FOUNDED.

It was not until June 30th that Fr. Junipero could accomplish the ardent desire of his heart, viz., that of going to San Diego. He went down in the packet-boat "Principe," and made the voyage in twelve days. He found there the two San Juan missionaries, and one who belonged at San Diego. His presence was consoling to them, and, being most anxious to go to work at once, he went to the captain of the packet, Don Diego Choquet, and asked him, in honor of San Diego, whose name he bore, that he would allow some of his sailors to aid in rebuilding the mission. The captain replied: "Not only the sailors shall help, but I will go myself as a common laborer." Elated by this satisfactory answer, the Ven. President wrote to the commandant, Rivera, asking him for some soldiers. The captain immediately detailed five of his sailors and a corporal to assist in the work.

Fr. Junipero, with two other missionaries, the marine officers, and twenty soldiers, with some laborers, set out for the spot where the mission had been. For two weeks they labored with such enthusiasm that hopes were entertained that, before the sailing of the ship, the church and the other buildings would be completed. However, the enemy of mankind could not bear to see the good work going on so prosperously, and accordingly he availed himself, not of poor ignorant Indians, but of the caprice of a Christian officer, to carry out his nefarious designs. On the 8th of September, Captain Rivera went to the mission and informed the principal officer that rumors were current that the Indians would again attack the mission, and that he deemed it necessary to retire with his men on board of his ship. The marine officer saw there was no ground to fear an outbreak, and he entreated Rivera to investigate carefully as to whether the rumor had any foundation; but the captain would listen to no reasoning, and insisted on carrying out his programme, to which Choquet reluctantly acceded, protesting that it would be a shame for the Spanish army to suspend work at the mere rumor of an outbreak. The latter officer communicated his views to Fr. Junipero, who felt his heart wounded as though it had been struck with an arrow, but he only said: "Let the will of God be done! He alone can remedy this evil." And he begged the Fathers to commit the affair to God in holy prayer.

The Viceroy, having been informed by Captain Choquet of the interruption in the work, felt it very keenly, and wrote immediately to Governor Neve, who resided at Loreto, requesting him to take up his abode at Monterey, and he ordered Captain Rivera to retire to Loreto. He informed Fr. Junipero of this decision in a long letter, written on the 25th of December, 1776. We will select a few extracts from it to show the zeal of this truly Christian Viceroy:

"The suspension of the Mission of San Diego must have caused a severe pain to your Reverence, as it has greatly displeased me, much more so as I am aware of the improper motives which caused it, which were made known to me by the Lieutenant of the Navy, Don Diego

Choquet. I suppose that, with the twenty-five soldiers sent to reinforce that Presidio, Don Fernando Rivera will devote himself to the erection of the Mission of San Juan Capistrano; but if he does not, the Governor of the Province, who has orders to reside at Monterey, will do it. I have ordered the Governor to have San Diego re-established, and not to punish the ringleaders of the last outbreak, hoping that they will themselves learn to regret their misdeeds. I likewise ordered him to erect the Mission of Santa Clara, in the neighborhood of the Presidio of San Francisco. The Governor, Don Felipe Neve, is directed to have recourse to your counsels, and to consult me in whatever is necessary to insure a happy result."

Had these letters reached our apostle in proper time, they would have spared him much trouble and anxiety. As it was, while waiting for them, he suffered a prolonged martyrdom. Although God tries his servants in many ways, they know that their suffering is but for a time, and when the storm is over, there will come a perfect calm. Twenty-one days after the work had been discontinued, there arrived from Lower California twenty-five soldiers, bringing two letters to Fr. Junipero. His pleasure knew no bounds, and he gave expression to it by the joyful pealing of bells, and the celebration of a high mass, on the following day, which happened to be the feast of St. Michael the Arch-Angel, and the patron of the Missions.

Captain Rivera, having received orders from his superior, liberated the Indians, whom he was going to send to San Blas, and detailed twelve soldiers as a guard to protect the workmen in the rebuilding of the San Diego Mission. He also sent ten of the military for a similar purpose to San Juan Capistrano, and left thirty at the Presidio; he, with twelve soldiers destined for San Francisco, went to Monterey, that he might not witness the re-establishment of San Diego, and the foundation of San Juan, to which enterprises he seemed much opposed.

Our zealous missionary, finding himself free to labor, went from the Presidio to the mission, with his neophytes, who toiled untiringly in rebuilding the mission. He wrote to the Viceroy, thanking him for his clemency to the poor Indians, and also for the reinforcement of soldiers. Then, together with Frs. Mugartegui and Amurrio, he proceeded to the place where the bells had been buried, and with the usual ceremonies founded the Mission of San Juan Capistrano.

In his zeal, he exposed his life to great danger. He went to San Gabriel to procure a few neophytes to assist at the buildings, and also to borrow some cattle. On his return, he took with him only one soldier and a Christian Indian. Having proceeded about ten leagues, they were suddenly overtaken by a multitude of savages, painted, and well armed with arrows. They shouted and threatened the Father and his two companions. The Christian Indian, in his native tongue, bade them beware, as many soldiers were approaching from the rear, which intelligence at once caused the assailants to drop their arrows, and even to become transformed into meek lambs. Fr. Junipero called them to him, made the sign of the cross on their foreheads, pacified and gained their confidence by giving them beads, and thus converted them from enemies into friends.

The Mission of San Juan Capistrano is situated in a lovely spot, from where the sea can be seen, and likewise the ships sailing by. There the Fathers devoted themselves to the cultivation of the vine, pomegranates, and other fruit; in a short time they had also good crops of wheat, corn, and beans, which supplied not only the neophytes, but even the soldiers.

With the aid of an interpreter, the Ven. President explained to the Indians that it was only for their good that the Fathers had come to live among them; and we are told that, while the Indians of the other missions were in the beginning over-anxious for bodily comforts, those of San Juan were solicitous only for baptism, asking it most earnestly from the missionaries, and finding the time required for preliminary instruction too long.

At the time of Fr. Junipero's death, that mission already numbered four hundred and seventy Christians; and afterwards the number increased so rapidly that in three months there were more natives baptized than during the three years and a half previous. Owing, no doubt, says Fr. Mugartegui, to the prayers of Fr. Junipero, who promised to continue, even after death, praying for the conversion of his dear Indians.

His zeal for the propagation of the gospel could not be satisfied; so, having re-established San Diego, and founded San Juan Capistrano, Fr. Junipero was anxious to learn whether the Mission of San Francisco had been established; for this purpose, after visiting San Gabriel, San Luis Obispo, and San Antonio, he arrived at San Carlos in the month of January, 1777, where the cheering intelligence awaited him that the Missions of San Francisco and Santa Clara had already been founded.

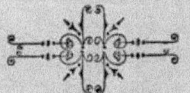

## CHAPTER XVI.

ESTABLISHMENT OF THE MISSION OF SAN FRANCISCO AND SANTA CLARA—WISE ORDERS GIVEN BY THE VICEROY—FATHER JUNIPERO VISITS THESE MISSIONS AND FOUNDS THE PUEBLO OF SAN JOSE.

During the stay of the Viceroy in Mexico, one of the favors which Fr. Junipero asked was permission to found the two Missions of San Francisco and Santa Clara. The zealous Bucareli promised to do all in his power, as soon as he could dispose of the troops required, and as soon as the way would be opened over the Rio Colorado.

We have seen that Captain Anza discovered a road from Sonora to California, and after having reported favorably, the Viceroy wrote to that officer to prepare himself for another expedition, and to try to raise thirty married soldiers, who, with their families, could settle and form a pueblo, and who would leave Mexico in the beginning of the year 1775.

In his letter of December, 1774, to Fr. Junipero, the Viceroy notified him of this second expedition; but this gratifying intelligence reached him by the packet-boat "San Carlos, as late as the 27th of June, 1775.

The marine officer of the Royal Navy had orders to survey the port of San Francisco, which he accordingly did, entering it at night, through what we now call the Golden Gate. That channel, says Fr. Palou, is three miles in length, and a mile and a half in width, with strong currents. They observed within the bay (which they called Mediterranean Sea) two arms of water—one running southeast for fifteen leagues, and the other four or five leagues to the north, within which they found a bay almost round, about ten leagues in width, where the great river of our Father St. Francis empties. All these bodies of water empty into the Pacific through the way called Farallones.

The packet remained there during forty days, and a barge, which was engaged in surveying the whole bay, had frequent communications with the Indians living along its shores. The captain, being asked if he thought it a good harbor, answered that it was not only one great harbor, but that it contained many, that several fleets could be anchored there, without the one knowing of the others being present.

A map and a description of this renowned harbor was forwarded to the Viceroy, who was more than desirous to have a mission established there at once. But the distance by land being nearly one thousand leagues, the expedition was not able to complete the journey within a short time. They were, however, at San Gabriel on the 4th of January, 1776, to which point, as we said in a previous chapter, the outbreak at San Diego obliged Captain Anza to repair.

Anza had orders to proceed to survey the port of San Francisco. After leaving Monterey, and in company with Lieutenant Moraga, he complied with this direction. Captain Anza impressed upon Captain Rivera the expediency of establishing these northern missions as soon as possible, and suggested that if he could not come up, he might send Lieutenant Moraga, reminding him that the settlers were weary of waiting at Monterey, that not being their destination; and having accomplished his commission, he, with ten soldiers, returned to Sonora to report to the Viceroy. Upon receipt of this letter, Captain Rivera sent orders to Lieutenant Moraga to accompany those who had come from Sonora to found the Presidio of San Francisco. A few days after this mandate was received, there arrived at Monterey the two packet-boats, "El Principe" and "San Carlos," the captain of the latter having instructions to go to San Francisco and aid in founding the mission.

Fr. Palou and Fr. Cambon were directed by their President to accompany the land expedition, which was composed of Lieutenant Moraga, a sergeant, and sixteen soldiers, all married, besides seven settlers, with their numerous families, servants, herders, and mule-drivers. The priests took with them two servants, two Indian neophytes of Lower California, and one from Carmelo to serve as interpreter, but he proved useless, as the Indians of San Francisco spoke a different language.

Four days anterior to reaching the harbor, they observed, in a great plain called San Bernardino, herds of cattle, seemingly of the bovine genus, which, however, were deer, or something similar to oxen, having horns so long that they measured sixty-four inches from point to point. The soldiers killed three of them, which were so large that a mule could not carry one but a very short distance. The flesh they pronounced delicious. They ran in the direction of the wind, and their large horns resembled fans. They saw, also, other smaller animals, called venado stags, of a bay color, besides herds of deer numbering two or three hundred, not larger than a buck of two or three years, with small horns and short legs, like the antelopes. It was difficult to tire them on the plains, but the soldiers succeeded in killing some by enticing them from the herds and pursuing them towards the hills.

The expedition halted in a place called even to this day Creek of Las Llagas de San Francisco, the dividing line between the Archdiocese of San Francisco and the Diocese of Monterey, and which is about eight miles north of Gilroy. On the 27th of June, they arrived in the neighborhood of San Francisco Bay, and pitched their tents, to the number of fifteen, on the banks of a great laguna which empties into the bay. The Indians soon came to visit them, manifesting all the demonstrations of peace, and bringing muscles and seeds to the men of the expedition.

The following day, under a shade of evergreens, Fr. Palou celebrated the first mass in honor of the Sts. Peter and Paul, whose feast the church commemorates upon that day. Here they remained an entire month, awaiting the arrival of the packet-boat. Each day the holy mass was offered, and they daily visited the rancherias, finding the Indians in every instance well disposed.

They surveyed the country around and found themselves in a peninsula from which there was no exit, except in a south or south-eastern direction. Fr. Palou says: towards the ocean we have an arm of the sea extending south-east, but land can be seen on the other side, this arm being only three leagues wide. In a northern direction we observe another arm of the sea towards the west and south, the Farallones are located and here also is the entrance to the harbor.

Whilst awaiting the arrival of the vessel, the missionaries cut timber near the mouth of the bay for the Presidio Mission, which latter was to be built near the Laguna on the plain. After waiting a month, Lieutenant Fagés seeing that no orders came from the Commandant Rivera, left six soldiers and two of the settlers in the place designed for the mission, and moved towards the entrance of the harbor.

At length, after a perilous voyage, the packet-boat arrived August 18th. All now went heartily to work and with the aid of the sailors a chapel and store house were erected at the presidio, and a chapel, store house and dwelling for the Fathers at the mission; the soldiers constructed barracks in both places, of timber, covered with tiles.

They took formal possession of the presidio on the 17th of September, feast of the Stigmata of St. Francis, patron of the presidio and harbor. Fr. Palou sang mass, blessed and erected a cross, and sang the "Te Deum," while the officers took possession of the place in the name of the monarch amidst the firing of cannon and musketry.

The taking formal possession of the mission was delayed to await orders from Commandant Rivera. Meanwhile the officers determined to explore the country around the bay and the river which empties into it. They fixed on a place of meeting. The captain of the packet "Quiros," with his pilot, Canizares and Fr. Benito Cambon, went with a barge to treat and become acquainted with the neighbouring Indians. They sailed north until a point was reached where the land expedition was expected.

On the same day the officer of the presidio, with a sufficient number of soldiers, proceeded to the south along the great bay till they reached the end of it. Here they were obliged to ford a river, to which they gave the name "Our Lady of Guadaloupe," and found themselves at the other side of the bay; instead of proceeding northward till they reached a point directly opposite the one whence they started, they followed a cañon, hoping thus to sooner join the barge party; but this was contrary to their expectations, for travelling with the cañada they came out on a large plain, far from the bay, and finding it impossible to meet their companions, they determined to follow the plain, where they found five rivers, all of which emptied into the bay.

They pursued their way along a great avenue of trees, and were stopped by a large river which they feared to cross, and they followed its course upwards, meeting many large rancherias of Indians, some of whom accompanied them, and pointed out the only place where the river was fordable. They observed that the Indians dwelt only near the banks of the river, their chief sustenance being fish and venison. Thousands of deer found pasturage on the plains.

The captain seeing that the time appointed for meeting the barge had already passed, resolved to return by the same route. Those who went by water having been detained by the non-arrival of their co-laborers, commenced a survey of the coast, and went as far as the mouth of the river which empties into the bay. Moraga in entering the rivers went as far as Suisun bay after crossing the San Joaquin, he found that the country was too extensive for his limited time, he observed here and there many little landings, and convinced himself after surveying the whole bay that it had no other communication with the Pacific than through the narrow channel or opening at present called Golden Gate.

Having finished their explorations they returned to the point of starting, and both officers sent reports of their survey to the Viceroy. Meanwhile, seeing that time for the packet to return to San Blas had arrived, and that orders to found the mission were not forthcoming, they determined to begin the establishment themselves. This was done, according to Palou, on October 9th. Some are inclined to believe that the mission was commenced on the 4th of the same month, it being the day on which the church celebrates the feast of St. Francis of Assisium, patron of the mission; but we are inclined to adhere to the authority of Fr. Palou rather than any other, supposing as it is probable, that on the 4th of October the land and water explorers had not returned, or that it was deemed prudent to wait a few days longer for orders from Captain Rivera; which reasons were sufficient to account for delaying the foundation, even though the feast of St. Francis would have suggested the idea of chosing the 4th of the month. At all events, we read in the life of Fr. Junipero Serra by the best authority—Fr. Palou—that the mission was established on the 9th of October and not on the 4th. Moreover the 9th being in the Octave of the Saint, was celebrated by the Franciscans with nearly the same solemnity as the feast itself. May we not suppose, that the Father seeing the mission was not established on the feast, would urge the officers to take the necessary steps within the octave of the festival. It is easy to suggest that there is a typographical error in the date, but if so, we can say the same of any other date given by Palou; if we accept his statement as correct on one page, we must proceed on the same theory throughout, unless there are very strong proofs of error. "After blessing the place, says Fr. Palou, erecting the holy cross, and forming a procession, at the head of which the image of our Fr. St. Francis was carried in triumph and then placed upon the altar; I sang the first mass and preached a sermon, regarding our holy Father as patron of the mission; officers, marines, sailors, soldiers and settlers from the presidio and mission assisted at the ceremonies, which were accompanied by a salute from numerous guns."

None of the Indians, says Palou, witnessed this solemnity, as in the middle of the previous month of August some left the peninsula and sailed to the deserted islands within the bay, whilst many crossed to the other side. Their departure was owing to a sudden attack made upon them by a tribe called Salsona, their mortal enemies, who, says Palou, live about six leagues distant to the south-east, near the arm of the sea; they burned their huts and killed a portion of the inmates and then retired; the soldiers were not able to arrive in time to prevent these depredations.

On this account conversions were retarded, the Indians not returning to the mission till March, 1777. The first baptisms were administered in June of that year. At the death of Fr. Junipero, nine years later, there were in that place three hundred and ninety-four Christians.

The natives around the mission were of a darker color, and more robust, than those from the other side of the bay. When any of their relatives would die, the men and women would cut their hair, and in their distress cover their heads and other portions of their body with ashes, as a token of sorrow—a practice observed in several parts of California. However, those on the south side did not cut their hair short; on the contrary, men and women, it appeared, had vanity enough to let it grow to considerable length, and when well combed they formed it into braids, and with this material the men manufactured a kind of turban, which they adorned with beads and trinkets.

Fr. Palou assures us that from San Diego to San Francisco, a distance of over two hundred leagues, they found not a single trace of idolatry, but only a negative infidelity. He observed, however, a few superstitious practices, especially among the old people, some of whom pretended to have the power to bring rain, or to produce good crops of corn. But such claims were not successfully imposed upon even these untutored aborigines.

When any of the Indians of the north fell sick, they imagined it was owing to the evil influence of an enemy, and would burn their dead; while those of the south, especially along the channel of Santa Barbara, were possessed of well-enclosed cemeteries, and always buried their dead.

The natives around the bay subsisted on seeds and field grass; it was the duty of the women to gather them when ripe, to pound them and make "atole," and with a kind of black seed they made a food similar to tomales, and shaped like an orange, and which was delicious, and tasted like roasted almonds. They also caught fish in abundance, all along the bay; gathered mussels, and hunted deer, rabbits, ducks, quails, and other game. Occasionally a whale would appear on the shore, and that was always an occasion of great rejoicing, as was also the capture of a sea-lion or walrus. They would slice and roast them underground; then hang them from a tree, and whenever hunger called they would help themselves until satiated. Along the cañons they gathered hazel-nuts, and on the sand-hills wild strawberries, during May and June. On the plains and hills abounded a kind of wild onion, which they also roasted underground, and called "amole." Fr. Palou, who often tasted it, pronounced it sweet and of as good flavor as ordinary preserves. There was another kind of "amole," of a saponaceous nature, similar to our castile soap; however, as Fr. Palou says, the poor Indians had very little use for it, as the men wore no other garments than those of Adam before the fall. To preserve themselves from the cold, which is felt here all the year round, especially in the morning, they used to daub themselves with mud, and as the day advanced, and the atmosphere became warmer, the coating was washed off. The women wore a kind of apron, made of skins, which reached just above the knees, and another, which they threw over their shoulders, to protect them from the cold. Their marriage ceremonies consisted in a mutual consent to abide together, till some disagreement occurred, when they would separate, and join with another. The children regularly followed the mother. They had no other formality of divorce than to say: "I put her out." However, Fr. Palou assures us that many had lived united to a good old age, loving their children tenderly.

They were very fond of their sisters-in-law, and even of their mothers-in-law; in fact, he who obtained a wife considered himself entitled to all her sisters, some having several wives, who, strange to say, dwelt beneath the same roof in harmony. Such was their miserable condition regarding marriage. But the influence of our holy religion was soon felt among them. A short time after the foundation of the mission, a man presented himself for conversion; he had four wives—three sisters and his mother-in-law—and at Fr. Palou's advice he left all except the first wife, and his example was followed by so many, that in a short time no one had more than one wife. Soon they became attached to the mission, and the missionaries provided for their support.

In the month of September, 1776, while at San Diego, Commander Rivera received a letter from the Viceroy, in which his Excellency intimated that the Missions of San Francisco and Santa Clara had already been established, when, in fact, nothing of the kind had been done; but, on the contrary, Rivera had retained with him the twelve soldiers designed for those missions. Concluding that something must be done, he started at once for Monterey, where he learned that, without his co-operation, the Mission of San Francisco had already been established. He accordingly proceeded to found that of Santa Clara. After crossing the plains then called San Bernardino, but now known as Santa Clara valley, he halted at the end of the bay, near a large river. The officers and Fr. Peña judged the place to be well adapted for a mission, and whilst Captain Rivera went on to visit the Presidio of San Francisco, the missionary remained in this place.

On the 12th of January, 1777, the soldiers and their families having come, Fr. Peña celebrated the holy mass, and established the mission. Soon the Indians began to call, and in May the sacrament of baptism had already been administered in many cases. An epidemic having broken out among the native children, many of them were baptized; so that, when Fr. Junipero died, Santa Clara contained six hundred and sixty-nine native christians.

This mission had many advantages which the others had not. It was situated in the plains of San Bernardino, which are from three to five leagues in width, and more than thirty in length. Its soil was very productive, and the crops of beans, corn, and other grains were abundant, and Fr. Palou assures us that he has eaten salmon of most delicious flavor, which was taken from the Guadaloupe river, which is not far from the mission. By means of irrigation they soon raised every kind of fruit. The Indians subsisted on acorns, oak trees abounding on those plains. The language used was similar to that spoken among the tribes near San Francisco. Traces of a sodomitical nature were observed here and in the other missions, especially along the channel of Santa Barbara; but the perpetrators, feeling ashamed, concealed themselves. Soon every vestige of such crimes disappeared before the influence of our holy religion; the poor natives, even before their conversion, used to say: "Such things were not right."

Fr. Junipero having returned to the San Carlos Mission in 1777, was most anxious to visit San Francisco and Santa Clara, as he had not been able to assist in their establishment; but he was obliged to postpone his trip until the arrival of the new Governor, Don Felipe Neve, who, on the 3d of February of that year, arrived at Monterey. Fr. Junipero pointed out to him how important it was that three missions should be located along the channel of Santa Barbara, and to this end they wrote to the Viceroy to solicit the necessary authorization. Meanwhile, Fr. Serra started for the north, and arrived at Santa Clara, September 28th. The next day being the feast of St. Michael the Arch-Angel, he sang mass, and preached. Proceeding northward, he reached San Francisco on October 1st, having made a journey of fifteen leagues, on foot, in one day and part of a night. He sang mass, and preached, on the feast of his glorious founder, St. Francis, in presence of the troops, who had come from the presidio, and the new adult Christian Indians, to the number of seventeen; thus rejoicing the hearts of the four missionaries. In order to recuperate from the fatigue of the long journey from Monterey, he remained at the mission till October 10th. In the meantime, he visited the presido, and gazing on the vast expanse of water before him, and seeing it impossible to proceed without embarking, exclaimed: "Thanks be to God! Already, our Father St. Francis, with the Processional Cross, has arrived at the terminus of California, since, in order to advance, it becomes necessary to embark." He alluded, no doubt, to the Catholic custom of carrying the cross at the head of all religious processions.

At the time the Ven. President visited San Francisco, there were eight missions founded, but at great distances from each other; and this circumstance caused him to remark: "This chain of missions is very much broken; it is requisite that the line be unbroken, that it may be pleasing to God and man. I have already solicited the foundation of three others, along the channel of Santa Barbara; help me to pray to God for success. After our wishes have been gratified to this extent, we will fill other vacancies."

Fr. Junipero's grand aim was the conversion of all the Indians who lived along the coast for two hundred leagues, and if there were several missions at reasonable intervals from each other, the unbelievers might, he thought, fall into the apostolic net, if not in one place, at least in another, and thus would the children of God and of His Holy Church increase from day to day. His mind being pre-occupied with these designs, he left San Francisco for Santa Clara, where he rested two days, and then continued on his route to San Carlos.

To facilitate the conversion of the Indians, his Excellency, the Viceroy, had ordered the new Governor to establish certain pueblos of Spanish people, whose avocations should be agriculture and cattle-raising. Neve having observed the extensive fertile plains south of San Francisco, established "el pueblo de San José de Guadaloupe," distant only about three miles from Santa Clara. There the settlers founded a town, now the city of San José, on the first day of November, 1777, giving them an "alcalde" or judge, and a few soldiers. The settlers were in the habit of going to Santa Clara to hear mass; and they soon raised fine crops of corn, wheat, and beans, which they sold to the soldiers, and with the profits of the business furnished themselves with clothing and other necessaries.

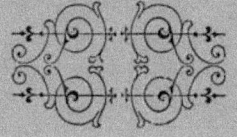

## CHAPTER XVII.

FATHER JUNIPERO RECEIVES FROM THE HOLY SEE FACULTIES TO CONFIRM—HE EXERCISES HIS NEW POWERS IN MONTEREY AND OTHER MISSIONS—NEW GOVERNMENT—DEATH OF BUCARELI—DIFFICULTIES.

When Fr. Junipero reached Lower California in 1768, amongst other papers, he found those informing him that the Jesuits had faculties to administer the Sacrament of Confirmation, and thinking he ought not to deprive his neophytes of the benefit of that great sacrament, and being desirous only for their spiritual interest, he wrote to his Guardian, to obtain for him or some other missionary that authority.

His Holiness Clement XIV. granted the petition on the 16th of July, 1774, for the term of ten years, which faculty duly authenticated was received by Fr. Junipero in Monterey, in the latter part of June, 1778.

Having perused carefully the instructions of the Sacred Congregation in regard to the use of this faculty, he began to exercise it immediately, and the next day being the feast of the Holy Apostles, Sts. Peter and Paul, having sung mass and given a suitable instruction on the sacrament, he confirmed some children, reserving the adults for a future day; he continued administering this sacrament till the 25th of August, when he sailed for San

Diego, where he confirmed the neophytes and the soldiers' children. From thence he proceeded north administering confirmations at all the missions, and he returned to Monterey on the 5th of January, 1779. His great humility caused him frequently to exclaim: "I always return edified at seeing how zealously they labor in the other missions, while we are always behind." Meanwhile, he continued his holy avocation of catechising and instructing. In June of that same year, he received by the frigate, the news that California had been taken from the government of the Viceroy, and that his Royal Majesty had appointed Don Teodore de Croix, Captain-General and Commander of both Californias, who was to reside in the Province of Sonora. This news naturally alarmed Fr. Junipero, who feared that the change might retard his contemplated missions; however, a letter to him from the Captain-General de Croix dispelled his fears.

From Queretaro that official wrote to Fr. Junipero: "The information I have received from his Excellency, and the contents of your letters to him, have persuaded me of your activity, zeal and prudence in the government of the missions, of your kindness towards the Indians, and your solicitude for their real happiness; at this date I have not at my disposal the help you ask, but I hope I shall be able shortly to satisfy your zeal, and to labor with you for the welfare of these establishments, trusting you will enlighten me with your advice and reflections. Your Reverence will find in me all that you desire for the propagation of our holy faith and the glory of religion. I beg your prayers and those of your religious for the happy issue of the important things confided to my care."

Queretaro, August 15th, 1777.

This letter assuaged, in a measure, the pain Fr. Junipero had felt at the change, but he soon found that there is not much reliance to be placed in human promises.

Some marine officers of the frigate, then anchored in San Francisco bay, were desirous to see our Apostle, and they wrote to him, requesting him if possible to go up to San Francisco. The Father begged to be excused, alleging his inability to comply with the request, on account of a swollen leg. Then Commandant Orteaga sent his two captains, with one of the surgeons of the royal navy, Fr. Palou being anxious to see his superior, accompanied them.

They arrived at the Mission of Santa Clara on the 11th of October; the very day on which Fr. Junipero arrived from Monterey, he had in the meantime changed his mind, and had resolved to go north to administer the sacrament of confirmation, and likewise to see the officers of the expedition. It is needless to say that all hearts rejoiced at so unexpected a meeting. Our good missionary was so much fatigued that he could no longer stand, having on foot, in two days, travelled twenty-seven leagues. When the surgeon saw his swollen leg, and sore foot, he declared that the accomplishment of the journey under such circumstances was miraculous. The next day the surgeon attempted to apply remedies, but Fr. Junipero entreated him to defer all treatment till they reached San Francisco, where he could rest. He walked that day as if his limbs were perfectly sound, and without taking any rest, and he also administered the sacrament of baptism to some adults, inviting the officers to act as sponsors. The ceremonies were very long, and sufficient to fatigue the most robust, and, in fact, the officers became wearied and expressed their astonishment at seeing our worthy missionary go through so much without any apparent inconvenience. They were highly edified by his devotion; and after remaining two days at Santa Clara they left for San Francisco. Before departing the officers tendered their congratulations and expressions of esteem to Fr. Junipero, who said, "I thank you gentlemen, and I shall endeavor to correspond to your good wishes, I shall confirm those of your crew who have not yet received the sacrament of confirmation." Accordingly, on the 21st of October, after singing high mass and making a suitable and fervent exhortation to those who were awaiting the reception of the sacrament, he confirmed the neophytes, soldiers and sailors who had not passed through the ceremony, and administered the sacrament during three days.

The surgeons again urged Fr. Junipero to allow them to treat his deseased limb, but he excused himself, saying he felt better, and that as the wound was very old, it would take too long to heal it, and that he would leave its care to his heavenly physician.

Nine days after the arrival of Fr. Junipero, the news of the death of the Viceroy Bucareli came, and also that war had been declared between Spain and England, which obliged the vessels to set sail at once for San Blas.

Fr. Junipero Serra felt the death of his benefactor and patron very keenly; however, trusting in God, he started for Monterey on the 6th of November, leaving there and in Santa Clara all the adults who were preparing for confirmation.

It was not without reason that Fr. Junipero dreaded the change in the government of the missions, and he daily lamented the death of the zealous Viceroy, who had so earnestly labored for their welfare.

Scarcely was the province of California separated from the jurisdiction of the Viceroy, than Fr. Junipero encountered obstacles and difficulties without number; he observed plans and regulations that were injurious to the welfare of the missions, he protested and explained himself, but it availed naught; the civil authorities were prepared to dictate, not only to soldiers, but also to the missionaries how the faith should be propagated. Fr. Palou tells us that he could narrate hundreds of these difficulties, but would mention only the prohibition to administer confirmation, with the very plausible excuse that the President in his faculty had not received the sanction of the Government authorities, though in reality it had been submitted to, and received the approval of the Royal Council to enforce it, with the suggestion that it should be enforced. Fr. Junipero remarked that for a year he had exercised this power, and the Captain-General had not objected. He presented his faculties to have them signed and approved by the officer, but DeCroix declined doing so, saying that the original must be presented. He also suggested that the President should not confirm till further orders. Fr. Junipero in his prudence abstained from exercising his faculty, fearing that should he administer the sacrament of confirmation contrary to the wish of the Governor, he might also be forbidden to baptize. He wrote to his Guardian in reference to his difficulty, who at once presented himself to the new Viceroy, asking a copy of the act enforcing the brief of the Pope, and the sanction for Fr. Junipero of the authorities of Mexico. The Viceroy wrote to the Governor not to interfere with Fr. Junipero, and to supply him with soldiers any time he wished to visit the missions. Whilst awaiting this decision Fr. Junipero occupied himself in catechising his neophytes. In September, 1781, the decision in his favor arrived, and having administered confirmation in San Carlos and in San Antonio, accompanied by Fr. Crespi, he went to San Francisco, to the great joy of Fr. Palou, who was now able to entertain his beloved President and his old confrere Fr. Crespi, who had not been in San Francisco since 1769, when none but roaming Indians were to be seen along the shores of the bay.

Here they remained till November 9th, and truly sad was the farewell of Fr. Crespi and Fr. Palou—a long farewell, since they were not to meet on earth. Infact, a few days after their return to San Carlos, Fr. Crespi was taken sick, and having received the last sacraments from the hands of Fr. Junipero, he died the death of the just, on the 10th day of January, 1782, being sixty years of age, and having labored thirty of these amongst the natives, sixteen among the Pames Indians, and the rest in California.

He was buried in the church of the mission, on the gospel side of the sanctuary, amidst the tears and bitter lamentations of the neophytes, among whom he had labored with such great zeal. Fr. Junipero appreciated him so highly, and so deep was his affection, that when dying, his last request was that he might be buried near Fr. Crespi.

Fr. Crespi kept a journal of his land and water explorations which is well deserving of perusal by those interested in the discovery of California, and the exploration of the Pacific Coast, as far north as the 55th degree of latitude.

## CHAPTER XVIII.

ESTABLISHMENT IN THE CHANNEL OF SANTA BARBARA—FOUNDATION OF SAN BUENAVENTURA—SAD OCCURENCE IN THE RIO COLORADO.

The letter of the Viceroy had such an effect on the Commander-General, De Croix, that even before he arrived at his destination he wrote to the Governor to send Captain Rivera to the "Aripes" to recruit seventy-five soldiers for the establishment of a presidio and three missions in the channel of Santa Barbara. One towards the north of the channel which was to be dedicated to the Immaculate Conception; one towards the south, dedicated to San Buenaventura, and a third in the centre, dedicated to Santa Barbara.

He purposed leaving fifteen soldiers at each mission, the remainder at the Presidio of Santa Barbara; moreover, he gave orders that families of Pobladores should accompany the missionaries for the purpose of establishing a town, to be known as "Pueblo de Nuestra Señora de los Angeles," near the river Portiuncula. At the same time he requested the religious of the College of Santa Cruz of Queretaro to found two missions on the Colorado river, to labor for the conversion of the natives, and to facilitate communication with California. These missions were founded on quite a different plan from that observed in California. They were without presidios, each having only eight soldiers and some settlers with their families; the missionaries were compelled to attend only to the spiritual welfare of the neophytes, who supported themselves as they had done before conversion.

Events soon proved how erroneous was this new method for the officers, soldiers and settlers were killed, and their wives and children retained as captives by the savages; the missionaries also were murdered, and al their stores burnt.

Captain Rivera having received orders from his superiors, began to recruit in Sinaloa, sending the recruits and settlers by sea to Loreto, from whence they were obliged to travel by land to San Diego Those whom he recruited in Sonora went with him along the Colorado river, taking more than a thousand head of horses and mules. Arriving at the Colorado, he found the two missions already established; perceiving that the animals were lean and sickly, and fearing they could not stand the journey of eighty leagues which lay between them and San Gabriel, he resolved to remain on the banks of the river until the stock should recover from this fatigue. He, together with a sergeant and six soldiers, belonging to the Presidio of Monterey, remained there, while under his direction the officers and soldiers, who had come from Sonora, under escort of an ensign and nine veterans from a presidio in Sonora went forward.

The Governor had already arrived in San Gabriel, and there he received the troops which had come from Lower California, and the detachment which arrived by way of the Rio Colorado. As the Governor expected none but Captain Rivera with the stud of horses, he dismissed the ensign and his nine veterans, who returned to Sonora by the same route followed in coming. They were told by

Indians whom they encountered on the way, that the two missions at Rio Colorado had been destroyed, and all the inmates killed by the savages; but this narrative was not believed until they reached the place, when they found a heap of ashes where the buildings had stood, and the bodies of the murdered priests and soldiers unburied, and being themselves attacked by the savages, they thought it prudent to return to San Gabriel, which they did after losing two soldiers and having one wounded. The Governor sent the same ensign and his seven brave soldiers, with letters for the Captain-General via Loreto.

This sad accident retarded the establishment of the missions along the channel. The Governor deemed it advisable to remain with his troops in San Gabriel, fearing an outbreak; meanwhile, he determined to lay the foundation of a Pueblo of Spaniards near the Rio Portiuncula, so called by the first expedition in 1769.

He united all the settlers, and gave them lands along the river, distant about twelve miles from the Mission of San Gabriel, he also gave a corporal and three soldiers to guard them, and in this quiet way towards the end of the year 1781, was founded the Pueblo entitled, "Nuestra Señora de los Angeles," a pueblo which one hundred years later counted its inhabitants by thousands, and bids fair to rival the first cities of the Pacific coast. The settlers commenced to raise crops of beans, corn and wheat, and thus supported themselves and families. Fr. Palou informs us that the colonists were obliged to travel a distance of four leagues to hear mass.

The Governor, Don Felipe Neve, arrived at Monterey February 3d, 1779, where he took up his abode; as a year and a half had passed since the assault and massacre on the Rio Colorado, and as no disturbance had occured in the interval, he determined while awaiting the ships coming with six missionaries recruits, that he would proceed to the establishment of the Missions of San

Buenaventura and Santa Barbara; and for this purpose he went to Fr. Junipero in February, 1783, to ask him for two missionaries. The President was busy with his neophytes, but being most anxious to see these two missions founded, and not having Fathers to dispose of, he cast his eye on Fr. Pedro Benito Cambon, who had lately arrived from the Phillippine Islands, in feeble health, and who was resting from the fatigues of his voyage at San Diego. He wrote, requesting him to meet him at San Gabriel, and leaving a missionary alone at Monterey, he started for San Gabriel, confirming in his way several christians in San Antonio and San Luis Obispo. As he passed along the channel of Santa Barbara, he rejoiced as he thought that soon the light of faith would illumine the numerous tribes living along its shores. Whenever he met the uncivilized objects of his attentions, he treated them with kindness and led them to believe that missionaries would at an early date come to live with them. Late on the 18th of March he arrived at Los Angeles, where he passed the night, and early the next morning he started for the Mission of San Gabriel, which was about four leagues distant; the journey seemed very long to him, fatigued as he was in body, and his mind oppressed with care and anxiety. Here he met the resident missionary and Fr. Cambon, who had come up from San Diego. It being the feast of the Holy Patriarch St. Joseph the day was celebrated with all solemnity; the bells rang forth a merry peal; mass was sung, and a sermon preached by good Fr. Junipero.

In the afternoon he visited the Governor, who returned the visit next day, when it was agreed to proceed at once to the foundation of San Buenaventura, and thence to Santa Barbara. Fr. Junipero was extremely anxious to conduct the solemnities of holy week at San Gabriel, but his wishes could not be realized, for it was announced that on the 26th of March, Tuesday in holy week, the expedition would start. During his stay at San Gabriel, which was about six days, he administered the sacrament of confirmation to many.

The San Buenaventura party set out after mass; it consisted of seventy soldiers, with their captain, commander for the new presidio, ensign, sergeants and corporals; also the Governor with ten soldiers of the company of Monterey, their wives and families, servants and neophytes. So numerous was the convoy that never had its equal been seen on any other similar occasion. It had but two priests, the president and Fr. Cambon. Fr. Junipero seeing such a concourse, could well say, as was said of the canonization of the Seraphic Doctor, "Quotandem tardius, eo solemnius," "the later it is, the more solemn it shall be."

This expedition left San Gabriel on the 26th of March, took a north-easterly course towards the channel of Santa Barbara.

They first halted at mid-night, when a messenger overtook them, bearing a letter to the Governor from Lieutenant-Colonel Don Pedro Fagés, who had just arrived at San Gabriel from the Rio Colorado. The Governor returned immediately to San Gabriel with his ten soldiers, leaving orders with the commanding officer to proceed, and in case he should not return at once, to establish the Mission of San Buenaventura, and to await there his arrival. This order was obeyed and those whom he had just left continued their route till the 29th, when they pitched their tents in a place called by the exploring party 69, "Assumpta," not far from the beach, where they discovered a large tribe of Indians, who dwelt in houses well built, and of a pyramidal shape. The day after their arrival they erected a large cross and prepared an altar under a shade of evergreens, where on the last day of March, on the feast of Easter, the Ven. Fr. Junipero blessed the cross and the place, and sang the first mass, preached to the soldiers a sermon on the Resurrection of our Divine Redeemer, and dedicated the mission to God under the patronage of St. Joseph.

The Indians manifested a very friendly disposition. They aided the soldiers in building a frame house for the missionaries, a chapel and barracks, fencing in all for greater security. By opening a ditch they brought water to the mission for daily use, and afterwards for the purpose of irrigating the soil. By means of a christian Indian, Fr. Junipero made known to the others the object of their coming amongst them. He remained here fifteen days, but had not the consolation of baptizing any of them. The following year, however, he met some christians there.

We will leave Fr. Junipero and those who accompanied him to San Buenaventura for a while, and follow the Governor to San Gabriel, to learn some particulars of the horrible massacre which occured on the Rio Colorado. Early on the morning of the 27th of March the Governor made his appearance at San Gabriel, when Fagés presented him with the instructions of the Commanding-General, to go with him to the Rio Colorado to punish the perpetrators of these terrible crimes. Our readers will thank Fr. Palou for having obtained from Fagés himself the juridical deposition of facts as they happened.

The nation of the Yumas inhabited the banks of the Rio Colorado. In the beginning their demeanor was peaceful, and they seemed glad to have the Fathers build the two missions which were there erected, one of which was dedicated to the Immaculate Conception, the other to St. Peter and St. Paul, and those were situated about three leagues distant from each other. Owing to the method of government adopted, the Fathers had nothing wherewith to win the Indians. It was difficult to bring them into subjection, coming as they did, to the mission only occasionally, and the Fathers were obliged to seek them in their rancherias; but despite these difficulties, a portion of the tribe was baptized.

Before long the unfortunate Indians perceiving that the cattle of the soldiers and settlers were devouring the grass and depriving them of the seed, by means of which they partially subsisted, and observing also, that the settlers had appropriated to themselves the few good spots along the banks of the river, where formerly they raised their crops of beans, corn, pumpkins and watermelons, they became so infuriated at the loss of their crops, and being instigated by the enemy of all good, who wished to destroy the missions, they determined to free themselves from the intruders by killing them; the Fathers had their fears, and consequently had for a long time tried to prepare all for the worst, and urged their congregation to receive frequently the sacraments of Penance and the holy Eucharist; also, to make the stations of the cross and recite rosary, so that their town seemed more like a convent than a secular establishment.

On Sunday at the conclusion of the last mass, many of the savage Indians simultaneously fell upon both missions, killing the four missionaries, who died exercising to the end their apostolic ministry, giving the absolution to the dying. They killed also the commanding officer, sergeant, nearly all the soldiers and settlers, except a few who concealed themselves; Captain Rivera and his soldiers fell, fighting bravely to the end. One of the soldiers escaping, fled to the Presidio of Sonora, where he reported the massacre, and was held as a prisoner till facts proved that his story was alas! too true. The General sent Colonel Fagés and some troops to the scene of slaughter, to deliver the captives and to arrest the culprits.

They arrived at the place, found the mission in ashes, the slain unburied, and among them the bodies of Fr. Juan Diaz and Fr. Moreno; not finding the bodies of the other two missionaries, Fr. Francis Garcia and Fr. Juan Barraneche, they supposed they had escaped, or probably that their lives had been spared, as Fr. Francis Garcia was very much beloved by the Indians, having lived amongst them several years. Whilst burying the slain, they noticed a spot where grass and flowers were growing, while the soil on all sides was parched and dry. They commenced to dig and soon found the bodies of the two missionaries, who had been buried by an old Indian woman, who was much devoted to the departed. They placed these remains in boxes and brought them to Sonora, confiding them to the President of the Missions of Pimeria, an institution then attached to the College of Queretaro.

Colonel Fagés was told that for several nights after the destruction of the mission, a procession of persons clothed in white, bearing torches and preceded by a cross, was seen going around the site of the mission; this so terrified the savages, that they fled to the delight of the poor captives.

Fagés following the course of the river, found the Yumas intrenched in the woods. He ransomed the captives, (purchasing them with clothes) and finding that it was impossible just then to punish anyone, he returned to Sonora to report.

The Commander-General gave him new orders to return to chastise the Yumas, and to secure the success of his enterprise, to go over to California with letters to the Governor, ordering him to go with all the troops he could spare to the Rio Colorado to aid Fagés in punishing the ring leaders.

The Governor deemed it advisable to wait till September for the execution of these orders. Fagés having ordered his soldiers who had remained on the banks of the river to withdraw, returned to San Gabriel to wait till September, when in company with the Governor and his troops, they set out for the Rio Colorado. But they destroyed but a few of the Yumas, and the road to California remained obstructed, and the Indians unsubdued.

The General and Governor were at length convinced that their method of subjugating the natives was inadequate, very expensive and produced no good results.

The Governor returned to the newly established Mission of San Buenaventura in April, saw that the Fathers were following the same old method as in the other missions, but said nothing. He soon set out again, and continued on his route till he reached the middle of the channel, some thirty miles north of San Buenaventura. Here he found a suitable place for a presidio near the beach, and in a place where the Indians were very numerous; at this point he ordered a cross to be erected, and Fr. Junipero said mass; the next day they commenced the erection of the most essential buildings, viz., chapel, store-house and barracks for the soldiers. Fr. Junipero remained here for a time, but learning that the mission would not be founded as yet, he resolved to go to Monterey, to wait for the missionaries, whom he expected to arrive on the ships which were expected. Meanwhile, in order that so many people should not be deprived of the holy mass, he sent one of the Fathers from San Juan Capistrano to minister to their spiritual wants, and he arrived at Monterey about the middle of June, to find that the vessel had reached that port on the 2nd of that month, bringing a letter but no missionaries.

## CHAPTER XIX.

LAST VISIT OF FR. JUNIPERO TO THE MISSIONS NORTH AND SOUTH OF MONTEREY.

---

As the new Viceroy, De Croix, had asked the Father Guardian for six missionaries for Upper California, and as six Franciscans wrote and offered to come themselves, Fr. Junipero supposed they would arrive by the ship which usually brought them provisions, but that vessel bore only a letter from his Father Guardian. And thus all his hopes of further religious progress were frustrated. It seems that when the new missionaries were in readiness to set out, they presented themselves to his Excellency to obtain from him the usual supply of church ornaments and agricultural implements. His Excellency replied that the agricultural implements were not necessary in the opinion of the General-Commander and Governor. The missionaries prudently investigated the motives which had lead to this refusal, and they learned that the three new missions had to be established on a different plan, similar to those on the Rio Colorado; so they resolved not to go to California, naturally concluding that the arrangement or design would eventually prove to be a failure. The Indians, being stupid and wholly carnal, were attracted to the mission first through an eager desire for food and clothing, and afterwards, though slowly, by higher motives; hence, if obliged to provide for themselves, as they had done before conversion, they would never become attached to the mission, but would fall off, and remain unbaptized.

This news, communicated by the Guardian to Fr. Junipero, afflicted him so much that we can safely assert it accelerated his death. However, he resigned himself to the will of God and his Prelate. The latter ordered him to suspend the foundation of other missions, but as Fr. Junipero had already established San Buenaventura, under the supposition that missionaries were coming, he began to deliberate whether or not he should recall the priest whom he had placed there; and being unable to determine the best course, he summoned the nearest missionaries, including those of Monterey, to a conference. There were at this meeting seven priests, and, after holding a consultation, they decided that the will of the Guardian could not have reference to the missions already in existence, but to those in contemplation. Fr. Junipero, in accordance with their decision, named the missionary who usually supplied his place when absent to go to San Buenaventura, as he was unable to leave his post. Meanwhile, he wrote to the Father Guardian, requesting him to send at least two missionaries to supply places, in case of sickness or death of those on actual duty.

Our Lord, who ever consoles the humble, sent him so many Indians asking for baptism, that entire rancherias presented themselves for instruction. His constant prayer was that the Lord would send laborers to His vineyard. As soon as the Father Guardian received our Apostle's letter, he approved of the establishment of the Mission of San Buenaventura, and sent two missionaries, who arrived at San Francisco, June 2d, 1783. From where, after resting a few days, they set out for Carmelo. There they found their Ven. President, sick from his running humor and from oppression of the chest. Fr. Palou tells us he suffered from this trouble of the chest from the time of his entry into the monastery, although he never complained, and when some of his religious advised him to apply some remedy, he used to say: "Let us leave it as it is; we might lose all." It is thus his life passes. He could have said with St. Agatha: "I have never applied any human remedies to my body." The same Fr. Palou gives us his opinion relative to the cause of this oppression. He says that Fr. Junipero, when giving missions, used to imitate St. Francis Solano, and scourge himself before the people with an iron chain, and whilst reciting aloud the act of contrition, he would strike his breast with a stone with such force that people were astonished that he did not break it. Sometimes, when endeavoring to describe the torments of a damned soul, in order to make a forcible impression upon his audience, he would take a lighted torch, and, laying bare his breast, would burn his flesh with it. The people were frequently moved to tears; whilst he would descend from the pulpit, apparently well and sound, and looking as though public penance did him no injury.

He was undergoing one of his most severe attacks when the last two missionaries arrived. Doubtless, the disappointment of not receiving help, and the delay in the foundation of other missions, increased the acuteness of the disease.

While still suffering intensely, and fit only to be in bed or confined to his room, the sight of the two missionaries revived him, and re-animated him with new courage. He left one of them, Fr. Diego Noboa, at Monterey, and with the other, Fr. Juan Riobo, started for San Diego, to administer the sacrament of confirmation, as the term of his faculty had nearly come.

The vessel left San Diego in August, and the oppression of his chest increased daily; so much so that all believed it impossible for him to attempt the voyage, and no one for an instant harbored the thought that he would be able to return by land and on foot. Fr. Junipero himself so believed, for, writing to Fr. Palou before embarking, he communicated to him his last wishes, and finished his letter in these terms: "I say all this, since my return will be only by letter. I feel so oppressed; pray for me." His zeal far surpassed his physical strength, and knowing that in July of the next year his faculty to administer confirmation would expire, he determined to make a last sacrifice, and visit for the last time all the missions, and confirm the neophytes.

He arrived at San Diego in September, his physical condition not improved. But this was only a new incentive to commence his apostolic labors at once. He administered confirmation, and immediately commenced a journey on foot of one hundred and sixty leagues to Monterey, allowing himself but a few days for rest at every mission. At San Gabriel his maladies increased, and all looked upon his death as inevitable.

The little Indian boy who served his mass, with tears in his eyes, used to say to the resident missionary: "The holy old Father wishes to die." The hearts of all were saddened at seeing him set out for San Buenaventura, as they feared he would not survive the journey; but Divine Providence aided and consoled him, and he had the satisfaction of administering confirmation to christians where the year before he found only heathens.

He traversed the channel of Santa Barbara, passing through many Indian pueblos, and, on seeing such vast multitudes of untutored people, he shed bitter tears, and cried aloud: "Pray ye, therefore, the Lord of the harvest, that He send laborers into His vineyard." (Matthew, 9th ch., 38th verse.) Beyond doubt, this sad spectacle, and the want of missionaries, shortened his days. The good missionary, full of merit, after confirming in Santa Clara and San Antonio, proceeded to San Carlos, and reached that place January, 1784, and, although in his seventieth year, he came not to rest, but to labor; he at once applied himself to catechizing his beloved neophytes. There he celebrated Holy Week, and after Easter set out for Santa Clara and San Francisco, to administer confirmation. He blessed the new church at Santa Clara, and on the fourth of May arrived at San Francisco. Fr. Palou embraced his beloved Prelate most tenderly, for he had feared that they would meet no more on earth. He enjoyed the anticipated pleasure of his company for a few days. But the joys of this world are ever transient.

Two days later, Fr. Palou was summoned to Santa Clara, where one of the missionaries was dangerously ill; he arrived in season to administer to him the last consolations of our Holy Religion, and received his last sigh on the 11th of that month. Fr. Antonio Murguia spent thirty-six years of his life in the conversion of the natives, twenty among the Pamés, five in Lower California, and the remainder here, leaving more than six hundred christian Indians whom he had baptized. He had just completed a large church, still standing, which Fr. Junipero pronounced to be the best he had seen in California. Fr. Antonio was not only the architect and superintendent, but also a common laborer, teaching the Indians how to work. His intentions were that Fr. Junipero should bless it on the 16th of May; but God called him hence ere his designs could be accomplished. Fr. Palou and Fr. Junipero were greatly attached to this fervent missionary; but the latter had not the consolation of assisting him in his last moments, as he was unable to reach Santa Clara before the 15th of May. He was accompanied by the Governor. That same evening the church was solemnly blessed according to the Roman Ritual, and the next day being Sunday, Fr. Junipero sang mass, preached, and confirmed.

As Fr. Palou was preparing to set out for San Francisco, his superior requested him to remain a little longer, and after having made the spiritual exercises of a retreat, for a few days, he with great contrition made a general confession of his whole life to Fr. Palou, who was greatly moved, more especially when he reflected that he would probably never again see his friend and President. However, God granted him the favor of assisting at the death of his beloved Father and superior.

Fr. Junipero employed the few remaining days of his stay in Santa Clara in baptizing and confirming his flock, going even to their houses when necessary, to administer the sacrament.

On his arrival at San Carlos, he sent his assistant, Fr. Noboa, to take the place of the good Fr. Murguria, and having done this, he continued to confirm applicants till the 16th of July, the day on which his faculties expired; and then, seeing that five thousand three hundred and seven souls had been confirmed, and that he could no longer confer the benefits of that sacrament, he said with St. Paul: "I have finished my course. I have kept the faith." That same day a government vessel, with provisions, arrived at San Francisco, bringing letters to Fr. Junipero from his Guardian, but no missionaries, as the College of Santa Cruz had then but few members. On reading this sad news, he saw his own death warrant. He immediately wrote to the distant missions, bidding the Fathers a last farewell, and requested those of San Antonio and San Luis Obispo to come up to visit him for the last time. He wrote to Fr. Palou, asking him also to come.

## CHAPTER XX.

EXEMPLARY DEATH AND IMPOSING FUNERAL OF THE VEN. FATHER JUNIPERO SERRA—HIS VIRTUES.

Although the Ven. President had not requested Fr. Palou's immediate presence, nevertheless he resolved to go, and finding that the boat was not to sail for some time, he started on foot, reaching the Mission of San Carlos, August 18th, to find his beloved Prelate very weak, though still able to walk every afternoon to the church, to teach catechism, to pray with his neophytes, and sing with them some verses in honor of the Assumption of the Blessed Virgin, as the church was then celebrating the octave of that feast.

Fr. Palou, hearing Fr. Junipero's voice, and recognizing it as natural, said to a soldier near by: "It does not seem as if our Ven. President were very sick." But the soldier, who had known Fr. Junipero since 1769, answered: "Father, we cannot rely upon such a supposition. This Holy Father is indeed unwell; but when there is praying and singing to be done, he always appears well, although he may be nearly dead."

Next day, Fr. Junipero requested Fr. Palou to sing mass in honor of St. Joseph, as he himself had been accustomed to do on the nineteenth of each month; and going to the choir, Fr. Junipero sang the responses, after which he recited aloud seven "Our Fathers" and seven "Hail Mary's" in honor of the great Patriarch, and in the afternoon he sang as usual in honor of the Blessed Virgin Mary.

The next Friday, he made the "Holy Way of the Cross," and afterwards treated of certain business appertaining to the missions. Fr. Palou found him pensive, in which state he always lived, especially since the expiration of his faculty for confirmation.

Five days after Fr. Palou's arrival, the packet-boat anchored in the harbor, and the royal surgeon hastened to Carmelo, to offer his services. He prescribed some burning applications, to which our Ven. Father replied: "Use as many of these remedies as you please." Not a murmur escaped his lips, though his sufferings were intense. He continued going about on foot, even distributing with his own hands food and clothes to the poor, naked Indians. On the 25th he expressed regret that the Fathers of San Antonio and San Luis Obispo had not yet arrived; he feared his letters had not reached them, which was really the case, they having been forgotten at the Presidio of Monterey. Fr. Palou, without delay, dispatched a courier to these Fathers, and requested them to come immediately, if they wished to see their beloved alive; but, though no time was lost, the good Father of San Antonio arrived only for the funeral, and the Father from San Luis on the seventh day, for the Requiem Mass.

On the 26th, Fr. Junipero arose, weaker than usual, and said he had passed a bad night, and wished to be prepared for the worst. All day he was buried in the contemplation of God, admitting of no distractions; at night, he repeated in tears his general confession, after which he partook of a little broth, then requested to be left alone.

The next day, very early, Fr. Palou found him reciting matins, as he was accustomed to do every morning, even while traveling. Being asked how he felt, he responded that he was well. "However," said he, "consecrate a host, and reserve it." After mass, Fr. Palou again visited the dying saint, who said: "I wish to receive the Holy Viaticum, but I will go to the church." Fr. Palou tried to persuade him to the contrary, assuring him that his cell could be prepared for the occasion; the saintly Father replied: "No; as long as I can walk to the church, there is no reason why our Lord should be brought to me." Fr. Palou was obliged to yield. Unassisted, Fr. Junipero proceeded to church, which was about three hundred feet distant from his room; he was accompanied by the officer of the presidio, the soldiers and Indians all deeply moved, and many bathed in tears.

On reaching the sanctuary, he knelt before a little table prepared for the occasion. Fr. Palou repaired to the sacristy, to vest and prepare for the administration of the Holy Viaticum. Upon emanating from this place, and when about to incense the Most Holy Sacrament, to his great astonishment he heard Fr. Junipero, whose voice resounded as clear and sonorous as when in perfect health, repeating the "Tantum Ergo Sacramentum," whilst tears bedewed his cheeks. The Viaticum was then administered to him, with all the ceremonies of the Ritual; after which our saintly Father remained kneeling, absorbed in God. Thanksgiving being concluded, he returned to his room, accompanied by his sorrowing children, some of whom shed tears of devotion, others tears of sorrow, knowing that they were soon to be deprived of a Father who so tenderly loved them. Alone in his room, he remained wholly wrapt in God.

Shortly afterwards, Fr. Palou, observing the carpenter of the presidio coming towards the room of the Father, asked him what he wanted; he replied that Fr. Junipero had requested him to make his coffin, and he wished to know how he would like to have it made. Fr. Palou then told the carpenter to make one similar to that which he had made for Fr. Crespi.

Our Ven. Father spent the entire day seated in his chair, in profound silence, taking no other nourishment than a little broth. At night he felt much worse, and asked for Extreme Unction, which he received seated in his chair, reciting with those present the Litany of the Saints and the Seven Penitential Psalms. He slept none, but spent the greater part of the night on his knees, or resting on the boards of his bed. When urged to lie down, he said he felt easier as he was. A portion of the night he passed seated on the floor, supported by some of his devoted children, with whom his room was thronged all night. They were induced to be present by the great love they bore their spiritual father. The surgeon, having been interrogated as to his condition, replied that he seemed to suffer much from prostration, but that the blessed Father wished to die on the ground.

Fr. Palou asked the dying saint if he desired the Plenary Indulgence, and having assented, he knelt, and with much fervor and consolation received this last great blessing of our Holy Religion, according to the Ritual of the Franciscan Order.

The next day, August 28th, he appeared to be much exhausted. The morning he spent seated in his chair, near his bed, which latter consisted of but hard, rough boards, covered with a blanket, which served the purpose rather as a coverlet. Even when traveling, Fr. Junipero used to lie on the bare ground, using his blanket as a pillow, embracing a large cross, which he brought from the College of San Fernando, and which he always carried with him. When not in bed, he placed the cross reverently on his pillow, and so spent his last night, refusing to go to bed.

At about ten o'clock, the officers of the frigate, with Captain Cañizares, whom he had known since 1769, and the Chaplain, Diaz, came to visit the good Father, who received them most kindly, rising from his chair to embrace them, and ordered the bells to be rung. Having taken their seats, they narrated many incidents of their voyage, and the notable events which had transpired since they had last seen him, in '69. After listening to them for a time, he said: "I thank you, gentlemen, for coming so great a distance, and after so long a time, to throw a handful of earth over my poor body." Hearing him speak thus, those present were astonished at his answering so well; and, concealing their tears, the officers said: "Father, we trust in God that you will recover, and continue your spiritual conquest." The dying saint, who doubted not his approaching dissolution, answered: "Yes, yes; do for me this act of charity, and I shall be grateful to you"; then, turning towards Fr. Palou, said: "I desire to be buried in the church, close by Fr. Crespi. When the stone church is built, they will throw me where they like."

Fr. Palou could not answer for a time, but when his emotion allowed him to speak, said: "Father President, if God is pleased to call you to himself, what you desire shall be done; I ask you my beloved Father, through the great love and kindness that you have ever borne towards me, that when you are in the presence of the Most Holy Trinity, you will adore it in my name, and do not forget me; ask God to bless all the inhabitants of these missions, especially those who are here present." "I promise," replied the Ven. Junipero, "if God in his infinite mercy grants me that eternal beatitude of which my faults render me unworthy, that I shall do so for all, and may it effect the conversion of many that I leave unconverted." Shortly afterwards he requested Fr. Palou to sprinkle holy water in his room, and being asked if he felt any uneasiness of mind, he responded in the negative, and having remained silent for a time, he suddenly exclaimed, "a great fear has come over me, I am much in dread, read the recommendation for the dying aloud, that I may hear it." "I did so," says Palou, "in presence of the officers of the ship and their companions, Fr. Noriega, the surgeon and many others." During the the recital our saintly Father seated in his chair, responded as if in perfect health. Scarcely had Fr. Palou finished, when the dying man full of joy, cried out: "Thanks be to God! Thanks be to God! the alarm has entirely left me, thanks be to God, there is nothing more to fear, such being the case, let us all go out. Much surprised every one left the room; animated by this triumph over hell, the captain of the ship said: "Father President, your reverence will see what St. Anthony can do, I have asked him to cure you, and I hope he will accede to my prayer, so that you may continue to labor for the welfare of the unfortunate Indians." The Ven. Junipero's only answer was a sweet smile, by which all understood that he did not expect to recover. Seating himself near the table, he took his diurnal and began to recite from it, when he had finished, Fr. Palou told him that it was after one o'clock, and requested him to take a cup of broth, which he did, and giving thanks he said, "let us go now to rest." He walked to his bed-room without assistance, took off his cloak and laid it upon his rough bed, and clasping his cross most reverently, seemed to be preparing himself for rest. Those present believed that he was going to sleep, as during the previous night he had not a single moment of rest. The officers went to dine; but Fr. Palou remained, and feeling uneasy, entered his friend's bed-room shortly after, and approached his bed, finding Fr. Serra in a position corresponding to that in which he had been left, but he was already sleeping in the Lord. No sign of agony was present and there was nothing to indicate death, save that he was breathless. "We piously believed," says Palou, "that he slept in the Lord just before two o'clock, on the afternoon of the feast of St. Augustine, in the year 1784, and that he went to heaven to receive the reward of his apostolic labors."

Father Junipero Serra died at the age of seventy years, nine months and four days. Nearly seventeen years of his life were passed in the world, and nearly fifty-four in religion. Thirty-five of these latter he employed in the apostolic ministry; occupied always in furthering the glory of God and the salvation of souls, and as Fr. Palou well remarks: " because he labored so well for others, we must believe that he did it also for his own sanctification."

As soon as Fr. Palou became satisfied that the Ven. President was dead he gave orders to the Indians to toll the bell, and when the mournful news was thus announced, everyone went to the room of the sainted deceased, and the crowd became so great, that it became necessary to prohibit further entrance. Clad in the same habit in which he died, Fr. Junipero's remains were laid in the coffin, ordered by himself the day before, and the remains were surrounded by six waxen candles. The doors were now thrown open, and the Indians tendered bouquets of wild flowers, which were deposited by the donors at the feet of the revered body, which remained at the same spot until night, constantly visited by the awe struck multitude. The devout touched his hands with rosaries, calling him "Holy Father," "blessed," and other names indicative of his virtue. About dusk the christian Indians, soldiers and sailors carried the body in procession to the church and placed it on a table, around which burned six wax candles. In compliance with the general demand, the door was left open all night, and devout groups took turns in watching and reciting rosary; two soldiers were put on guard, and though strict orders were given that no one should touch Fr. Junipero's body or habit, nevertheless, the next day it was found that several pieces of his habit had been removed, and also portions of his hair. On Sunday, August 29th, a solemn Requiem mass was sung, at which were present the Captain of the packet-boat, the marine officers, the Chaplain, Diaz, and military. Every half-hour cannons were fired and the funeral bells tolled mournfully.

Fr. Sitjar of the Mission of San Antonio reached Monterey on the morning of the funeral, and hearing there of the death of his beloved superior, celebrated mass, and immediately afterwards set out for Carmelo, together with the Adjutant-Inspector of both Californias to represent the Governor, who was absent.

The church, though large, was crowded; the office for the dead was chanted, and Fr. Palou sang the solemn Requiem mass, at which latter the officers assisted, bearing lighted tapers all the while. After mass a solemn dirge was chanted, and the burial was left for the afternoon.

At four o'clock an impressive funeral procession was formed; the remains were borne on the shoulders of the officers, who all deemed it an honor to be permitted to carry the body of the holy man. The other officers and the soldiers and the sailors bearing lighted tapers, preceded the coffin, lastly came the "Celebrant in Cope," accompanied by Deacon and Sub-Deacon. They moved slowly and solemnly around the plaza, pausing four times to repeat a dirge, which in Spanish is called "Posas."

On arriving at the church, the remains were again placed upon the table, lauds were sung, according to the Franciscan manual, and then the mortal remnants of the great Fr. Junipero Serra were laid to rest in the sanctuary at the gospel side. The mournful ceremony was concluded by a solemn dirge, but the voices of the chanters were drowned by the sighs and sobs of the multitude.

The funeral over, all gathered around Fr. Palou, eagerly asking for relics, and not having wherewith to satisfy all demands, he gave one of the under-garments of Fr. Junipero to the captain of the packet-boat, that scapulars might be made for the sailors from it, and he further signified his intention to bless and distribute these relics on

September 5th, the seventh day after the funeral; and on the appointed day he presented to the soldiers and others interested, portions of the Father's under-garments, and to the Royal Surgeon he gave one of his handkerchiefs, which that officer declared would cure more people than ordinary medical remedies, and indeed, later on the same pious and scientific man stated that through the handkerchief a poor sailor, who was suffering from a violent headache, had been cured by simply applying it to the affected part—and when this had been done the sick man slept, and thereafter arose perfectly sound. Fr. Antonio Paterna of San Luis Obispo, though he made all possible haste, did not arrive until three days after the death of his beloved prelate, and being advanced in years, having attained the age of sixty, and owing to the fatigue of the journey and the intense heat, he fell dangerously ill upon reaching Carmelo. Fr. Palou feared his death, and therefore he prepared him for the end, leaving, however, the administration of the Holy Viaticum for the next day. He suggested to the invalid, the idea of girding himself with a hair cloth, belonging to Fr. Junipero, which he accordingly did, and the next morning found him so well that the last sacraments were not administered, and in a few days he was as well as usual. Fr. Palou in referring to these and similar cases, is careful to inform us that he does not intend to declare them miraculous, but merely to show the very great esteem in which they all held Fr. Junipero. The soldiers frequently asserted that at whatever hour of the night the guard was changed they always heard him praying.

Fr. Palou, desirous to manifest love and respect for his prelate, was not satisfied with having had a solemn funeral, but on the seventh day, he again caused mass to be said, at which the officers, soldiers, sailors and Indians assisted, as they had on the day of the funeral, and during these inspiring ceremonials cannons were fired every half-hour, as at the death of a General. After mass he blessed the scapulars made of the tunic of Fr. Junipero and distributed them among the soldiers, telling them not to consider them as relics, but only as things blessed by the church, and as mementos of the virtues of the holy man who had worn the garment. He also distributed some medals belonging to the deceased, and the congregation departed satisfied. The Commanding-officer selected for himself the sandals of the poor Franciscan.

Then Fr. Palou, in sad accents, deplored the loss of his amiable Father, prudent prelate, and wise and exemplary teacher. These and other acts of Fr. Junipero, says Palou, which are related in this historical sketch, are so glorious in themselves that we can never forget him, and the memory of his name shall remain not only among his children, but amongst all the inhabitants of California.

So that if I did not fear being charged with a disciple's partiality towards his teacher, knowing that he, despising the world and its pomps, buried himself in the wilds of California, his mind occupied only with plans for conversion of the natives, I would nevertheless, not hesitate to apply to him what Solomon says of a wise man: "His memory shall not recede, and his name shall be looked for from generation to generation."

His works have made a lasting impression upon the inhabitants of Upper California, where he labored so zealously during sixteen years, leaving at his death fifteen settlements, six of Spaniards and nine of natives, all baptized by him or by his companions. The number of christians in Upper California when he closed his labors was five thousand, and if we count those of Lower California, there were seven thousand.

In his last moments, Fr. Junipero promised to pray for the conversion of the misguided Indian, and Fr. Palou assures us that the number of converts increased so rapidly that Fr. Mugartegui wrote from San Juan Capistrano: "During these last four months we have baptized more Indians than in three years previous, and we ascribe this great increase to the intercession of Ven. Junipero Serra, as they have come unsolicited to ask for baptism, and in numerous instances they have come from afar, and speak a language different from that used by the Indians of this mission." And the other Fathers might have borne testimony as to the same marvelous increase, for, says Palou, in the report they sent to me at the end of that year, I observed that in the four months following the death of Fr. Junipero, in the various missions, nine hundred and thirty-six baptisms had been registered, the number never before being so great. He concluded the eulogy of his beloved master with the words of Holy Writ: "The memory of the just shall live forever." (Ps. iii., verse 7.)

That Fr. Palou was not mistaken we can testify, for now one hundred years after the death of Fr. Junipero, we hear his name pronounced with love and respect, not alone by Catholics, but even by those of other denominations; and we see protestant papers copying with avidity sketches of his life, and able pens writing in select magazines interesting accounts of his labors and the missions founded by him. Let us in conclusion lay on his tomb a bouquet of his many virtues, which will not fade as do those made of natural flowers, which to-day are fresh and to-morrow withered.

The life of Fr. Junipero Serra, resembles one of California's lovely fields in spring-time, adorned with variegated attractions. The virtue which shone most conspicuously in him was profound humility; though a great preacher, he never referred to his sermons, and always considered himself inferior to others; when made master of novices, he looked upon himself as a novice. shunned all distinction, and only through obedience accepted the office of President of the missions, and fearing the influence of some dignitaries at Madrid, he forbore writing to them lest he might be compelled to accept other ecclesiastical dignity. He was remarkable for the prudence which he manifested in all his dealings, religious and secular, never assuming the responsibility in difficult cases, but consulting his Guardian and Counsellors. In governing the missions, a missionary could well say as was said of Elias, that he lay down and rested under the shade of a Juniper. (3d Bk. of Kings, 5th verse.) "He cast himself down and slept in the shadow of the juniper tree."

His obedience was truly sublime, he honored and obeyed each superior, even in the most trivial things; his charity was so great that no one feared for their reputation or good name; whenever in the conversations wherein he took part, he observed that there was danger that the precepts of charity would be forgotten, he said: "Let us not talk of this, it is painful to me." Hence the natural virtue which Plinius attributes to the juniper tree we can apply to our Junipero, namely, that the former grows in the wilderness and the snakes flee from its very shadow, so that men may sleep securely beneath its shade.

He had no other enemies than those of God, and those who impeded the subjugation of the natives; the former he strenuously endeavored to convert, and towards the latter he never evinced any resentment, but eventually won them to his side by his prudence, kindness and patience; on seeing any of his plans thwarted, he would only say: "God wills it so, the time of the harvest has not yet arrived for us." The officer whose conduct obliged him to undertake a long and painful journey to Mexico, in order to obtain favorable dispositions for these settlements, being recalled to Mexico, feared that he might not be received kindly by the Viceroy, and availed himself of the influence of another missionary to obtain a letter of recommendation, and

Fr. Junipero gave it so willingly, that when the officer arrived at Mexico his reception was most gracious, and he obtained a promotion to captaincy.

His charity towards the poor was so marked that he employed not only his salary, but the alms for masses, and he would even go without food for the purpose of enabling him to contribute to the needy; with his own hands he fashioned their under-garments, and sought to teach the savages to make and repair them. Only four days before his death, an old Indian woman, eighty years of age, came to see Fr. Junipero, and in the presence of Fr. Palou, the holy, dying man came from his bed-room, bearing a blanket which he presented to his aged visitor. After his death it was discovered, that to supply her, he had remained with but half a blanket. In his diet he was most frugal, he never ate meat, contenting himself with fish and fruit, which were, he used to say, the nourishment of the Mother of God. He slept little, spending the greater portion of each night in prayer and contemplation. He displayed an admirable spirit of fortitude in the many trials and difficulties with which he was surrounded in establishing the missions. When the missionaries were about to abandon San Diego and return to Lower California, Fr. Junipero resolved to remain there alone. With equal fortitude he overcame the obstacles incident to the task of rehabilitating that mission.

His faith was lively and constant, and his hope firm, hence he employed his whole lifetime in propagation of the holy faith in which he so firmly believed, and was ever ready to shed his blood in its defence.

At one time a false rumor alarmed the soldiers and missionaries at Monterey, and Fr. Palou tells us, that although the report was not fully credited, still the soldiers were uneasy. A few days after the savage massacre of San Diego, an Indian woman, who was a christian, went trembling and weeping to the corporal, telling him that the Zanjones were coming down the cañon in great numbers, and well armed, as if ready to fight. As soon as the corporal heard this, without examining whether the statement was true or otherwise, he sent word to the officer of the presidio, who mounted his horse and came with his troops to protect the mission. Filled with joy at the prospect of giving his life for Christ, Fr. Junipero communicated this news to his priests. Behold! Fathers and companions, said he, the long desired hour has arrived; they tell us the Zanjones are here, and we have but to reanimate our courage and prepare for the worst. Going out they saw the troops preparing for defence; the danger to which they were exposed was indeed great, since they resided in six different huts, built of pales or lumber and thatched with tiles, thus forming a very inadequate protection. It was suggested to the President, that during the night all should sleep in an adobe room which served as a blacksmiths forge. The Fathers accordingly took shelter in this retreat, and passed the night in listening to narratives of the many encounters Fr. Junipero had had with Indians. When morning dawned no Zanjones could be seen. Either the rain, which fell heavily that night, prevented their coming, or the Indian woman only imagined the danger.

Fr. Junipero was a devout client of St. Joseph, as we have already had occasion to see; he was also devoted to St. Bernardine of Sienna, having obtained through the intercession of that saint the cure of one of his neophytes at San Carlos, who had been nearly crushed to death under a pine tree which had fallen upon him. He had the facts relating to this incident painted on canvas, and placed in the church for the edification of new christians.

His zeal for the decency of divine worship and for all that pertained to the celebration of the mysteries of the

Catholic church was undeniable, and was shown by his solicitude in having the sacristies well replenished with sacred vestments and vessels; by his instructions to his missionaries to ask something for the service of the altar, when writing to Mexico; and by the great solemnity with which he kept the feasts of our Lord and the Blessed Virgin Mary, and by the fervor which he displayed when preaching. Having heard that Pope Clement XIII. had ordered the preface of the Most Holy Trinity to be sung or said at mass on those Sundays that had no proper preface, he was overjoyed and exclaimed: "God bless the Pope, who has ordered such a devout preface! Would to God that the feast of the Most Holy Trinity were raised to double the first class, that we might in imitation of our Father, St. Francis, celebrate the office of the Most Holy Trinity with a solemn feast." When the Indians sang the "Tota Pulchra es" he shed tears of devotion. He also displayed similar feeling during the singing of the Passion in Holy Week; and upon Holy Saturday his emotion was so marked that he was unable to sing the "Gloria," and many were the tears he shed in the recitation of the stations of that Holy Cross which he had erected throughout California.

Fr. Palou finishes the chapter reciting the heroic virtues of this servant of God, with the remark that the last words of Fr. Junipero Serra to him and to all the bystanders were: "Let us go to rest." We trust and believe that his soul is now resting in God, in the company of St. Augustine, the great Doctor of the church, whose office he recited a few moments before expiring. Before concluding we will say something of the resting-place of the mortal remains of the hero of these pages.

## CHAPTER XXI.

MISSION OF CARMELO, ITS RUINS AND ITS RESTORATION.

The greatest ambition of Catholics is to be buried in consecrated ground, and even those who are lukewarm fear nothing so much as to be deprived of christian burial, a punishment which the church inflicts only on those who die in a duel, or commit suicide, or who are public and scandalous sinners, refusing to receive the sacraments and to be reconciled to the church. But the most cherished desire of the Catholic is to be allowed the privilege of being buried within the actual precincts of the church, a privilege which was at first granted only to holy martyrs, but which became very common in the middle ages. But the honor of being buried inside of the sanctuary has been always reserved to bishops and priests, and it has been considered proper that they should find their final resting-place as close as possible to that altar where they so often offered the Immaculate Lamb of God. We are not astonished, then, that the saintly Junipero had only one request to make before dying, namely, to be buried in the sanctuary, near his fellow-laborer and companion, Fr. Crespi. This wish was carried out by Fr. Palou, as is testified in the Records of the Dead, kept to this day in the church of Monterey, and which reads as follows:

"On the 29th of August, 1784, in the church of this Mission of San Carlos de Monterey, in the 'Presbiterio'

(sanctuary) on the gospel side, before the altar of our
Lady of Dolours, the office of the dead having been
recited, and High Requiem Mass having been sung, with
all the accompanying ceremonies and functions prescribed
in the manual of the order for the funeral of the religious,
with the assistance of Brother Christoval Diaz, chaplain
of the packet-boat San Carlos, anchored in this port, and
the Rev. Fathers, Preachers, Friars Buenaventura, Sitjar,
Minister of the Mission of San Antonio, and Mathias of
Santa Catalina, Minister of this Mission. I gave ecclesiastical burial to the body of the Rev. Father Lecturer,
Friar Junipero Serra, President and Founder of these
Missions, who was born in the Holy Province of Mallórca,
where he took his habit, on the 14th of September, 1730,
aged nineteen years, two months, and twenty-one days,
where he proved himself to be a true and learned
religious, and where he taught with great success the
philosophical course, I having the honor to be one of his
scholars. When that course was finished, he was appointed Professor of the First Class of Sacred Theology,
in the University of the Island of Mallorca, and was there
honored with the tassel (borla) of Doctor of that Faculty.
Having filled the Professor's chair to the satisfaction of
the University and the Holy Province, he was universally
considered uncommonly learned and eloquent in the pulpit, and attracted the attention of both universities, which
institutions recommended and praised his sermons as
being of the greatest importance. Highly and generally
esteemed, and enlightened by God, he renounced those
honors which were offered him, and those which he had a
right to anticipate, and sought to employ the talents
which God had given him in the conversion of the Gentile
Indians. Having obtained his superior's permission, he
joined in the year 1749 the mission which was then in
Cadiz, and which was destined to promote the propagation of the faith through the Mission of San Fernando, in
Mexico, at which latter place he arrived on the first day

of January, 1750. He remained in that college till the beginning of June of the same year, when he was sent to the Mission of Sierra Gorda (which had been founded for six years), and where he worked with watchfulness and zeal, and served as a christian exemplar. Nine years after he was recalled from his missionary charge, to preside over the contemplated establishments at the river San Sabá, which were, however, frustrated by the death of the Viceroy. He remained in the college, employed in giving missions. He likewise assisted in the duties of the Sainted Tribunal of the faith, in accordance with the orders of his commissary, discharging this service to the satisfaction of the tribunal. In administering the missions amongst the brethren, he remained till June, 1767, when he was called by the Rev. Father Guardian of the college, and named President of the sixteen Missions of Old California, which had been controlled previously by the Rev. Fathers the ex-Jesuits. He remained one year in Old California, the Missions of Loreto being under his charge. During that period he visited those institutions several times, comprising within his journey those located both to the south and north of his abode as well. In April, 1769, he left Loreto, with a land expedition, in search of the port of San Diego, and arrived at the frontier of Ancient California. On his way he founded the Mission of San Fernando de Villacatá. Arriving at the port of San Diego, he rested there whilst the expedition went to look for the port of Monterey. He founded the Mission of San Diego, in 1769. He then went up by sea for the purpose of discovering Monterey, and aided in founding this mission. He continued, as circumstances would permit, to build up the remainder of the missions, as may be seen at the present time in the parochial books of foundations. During fourteen years of his life in California, he traveled much. He once went to Mexico, to procure means for these spiritual conquests; while, during the rest of his travels, he visited the California missions, striving to animate his dependants with zeal and prudence. His visits were made oftener after he received the authority to confirm, which his zeal caused him to solicit. Within the period during which he exercised that faculty, he confirmed 5,307. About one month and a half after the expiration of his powers, he delivered up his soul to his Creator, at the age of seventy years and nine months, less four days, having been an apostolic missionary thirty-five years, four months and a half. He prepared himself for death by making a general confession, as he had already done several times. Finding that the complaint in his chest was getting worse, and that he had some fever, on the 27th of the month he went on foot to the church. He there received the last sacred rites on his knees, to the edification of the people, and in their presence received the Holy Viaticum, as ordained in the Roman Seraphic Ritual. When the ceremony commenced, the Father was on his knees, chanting with his sonorous voice, and to our astonishment, the 'Tantum Ergo.' In the same posture he gave thanks to our Lord; after which he returned to his room. At night he asked for the holy oils, and repeated with us the Penitential Psalms and the Litanies. The remainder of the same night he passed giving thanks to God, sometimes on his knees, and sometimes sitting on the floor. He did not take to his bed, but was always dressed in his habit and cloak. At the break of day he asked me to give him the Plenary Indulgence, which he received kneeling. On the morning of the 28th he was visited by the captain of the bark, Don José Cañizares, and chaplain. He received them sitting, expressing gratitude for their visit. He embraced the chaplain, giving thanks to God that, after traveling so much, they had arrived at last to throw a little earth on his remains. A few minutes after making this remark he said that he felt some fear, and asked me to read aloud the recommendations for the soul, which I did. He then responded as if in good health, and exclaimed with de-

light: 'Thank God! I am now without fear, and have
nothing to dread. I feel better; let us go out.' He then
arose, and afterwards sat down at the table and took a
little broth. He then wished to rest, taking nothing off
but his cloak. He laid tranquilly for a time, and then
rested in the Lord. Without making any further sign he
delivered his spirit unto the Creator, a little after two
o'clock in the afternoon of the 28th, the feast of San Augustine, Doctor of the Church. When the bells began to
toll, the little town was in a state of commotion; the
Indians cried, lamenting the death of their good Father,
as likewise all the people, whether on shore or on board
the ship. All asked for a remnant of the habit he had
worn. They even went so far as to cut within the church
pieces from the habit in which Fr. Junipero died. Before
death, he ordered (without letting any of those present
know of it) the carpenter of the presidio to make his coffin.
We promised, if the multitude would hold their peace, to
devote a tunic of the deceased Father to scapulars for
their benefit. Notwithstanding this, those who guarded
the body in the church appropriated locks of his hair as
keepsakes. This they were induced to do because of their
regard for the departed. His funeral was attended by
every one, whether on shore or aboard ship, each one
doing what he could in honor of the deceased Father.
The captain of the bark utilized his artillery in conferring
upon the deceased all the honors of a General, and the
Royal Presidio of Monterey responded to the salute. The
same marks of respect were repeated on the 4th day of
September, with vigil and high mass, at which the same
people attended. Upon this occasion another clergyman
officiated, namely, Rev. Fr. Antonio Paterna, minister of
the Mission of San Luis Obispo, who could not arrive in
time for the funeral. And that everything said may
appear of record, I sign this in said mission, on the 5th
day of September, 1784.

        FR. FRANCISCO PALOU."

Have not the facts we have translated from the Records of Death been already told in the life of Fr. Junipero; and if so, why are they repeated now? I answer by simply saying that I have been requested to insert them in this book as a recapitulation of what has been described in detail. Owing to the concise manner in which these facts are thus given, newspaper reporters and tourists have frequently commented upon and copied them. Before concluding, it may be proper to answer the question as to what became of that church of stone, of which Fr. Junipero spoke when, just before dying, he requested Fr. Palou to lay his body close by that of Fr. Crespi, remarking: "When they build the church of stone, let them throw me where they like." Can we for a moment suspect that his religious friends had so little respect for his memory as to let him be buried outside of consecrated ground? By no means. Why, then, is no notice taken of the removal of the remains of Fr. Crespi and Fr. Junipero from the old church to the new one? It is the general opinion of the old residents of Monterey that the new stone church, alluded to by Father Junipero, was built on the same spot where the old edifice stood, and according to this supposition the graves of the two first missionaries remained undisturbed and enclosed within the sanctuary of the new church, on the gospel side, as they were in the temporary building. It is to be regretted that nothing can be found in the old records of that parish concerning the year of the construction of the new church; but it is believed that it was soon after the death of Fr. Junipero, and before the close of the last century. The church of stone remained in use till after the mission was secularized; then it was abandoned, and modern vandals began to demolish it, and to take beams and materials from it to aid in building their farm-houses. The author has been told that about the middle of this century $500 would have repaired the church, and thus preserved to our time the beautiful monument of Carmelo. But that sum was as difficult to obtain in those days as $15,000 would be now, which latter amount would be necessary to make the needed repairs. Those who are not acquainted with the facts blame our ecclesiastical authorities for having permitted this and other mission buildings to go to ruin, but such critics forget the thousand difficulties by which our superiors were surrounded, and the thousands of dollars they were forced to expend in order to reclaim these very missions from the hands of those who, without right, settled upon the mission lands. While lawsuits were pending, storms and rapine were working havoc on these sacred walls, so that when justice was done, and the missions restored to their proper owners, some of them were in ruins, and our Bishops found themselves heavily in debt, mainly on account of these protracted law-suits. They were pressed, also, by the urgent demands for more churches and schools in the central locations. In some places, as in Carmelo, the old church is far from the modern town, and of no use except as a reminder of days gone by.

Having visited the ruins of Carmelo many times during the last twenty years, the author, each time, has seen additional signs of decay and ruin. The present pastor of Monterey, the zealous and energetic Very Rev. A. Cassanova, V. F., has sought, since he took charge of Monterey, in 1868, to save Carmelo Mission, but owing to the fact that the town has decreased in importance, it is now scarcely able to support its pastor; and had he not means of his own, his situation would, at times, not be a pleasant one. How, then, could he afford to spend thousands in the reconstruction of the old mission? He has, from time to time, appealed to the public, but in vain. Seeing, however, that a more propitious occasion than the first Centennial of the death of Fr. Junipero Serra could not be found to make another effort to save the Mission of Carmelo, with a determination peculiar to his character, he has taken the work into his own hands, and before these lines will appear in print he will have spent the last cent of his savings. Trusting in the generosity of the few who will follow his noble example, we cherish the hope that the walls of the old church will be protected, the sacred precincts roofed in, a new altar erected, and that when the 28th of August of this year 1884 arrives, we will hear once more within those sacred precincts the voice of the minister of God begging eternal rest for the souls of Frs. Junipero Serra, Crespi, Lopez, Louzen, and for the souls of the Governors who are also there buried.

I close my life of Fr. Junipero Serra, fondly wishing that before it appears in print, a marble slab will show us the spot where lie the mortal remains of the President of the California Missions; and let us hope that the present Pastor of Monterey, who, in 1882, succeeded in finding the bodies of those four priests buried in Carmelo, will be rewarded by further identifying the mortal remains of the hero of these pages, which have been written only to perpetuate the memory of a poor Franciscan, who left honors, relatives and friends to spend his life in laboring for the conversion of the Aborigines of Alta California.

# CONTENTS.

### CHAPTER I.

Birth, studies and religious profession of Fr. Junipero Serra ................................................... page 5

### CHAPTER II.

Serra solicits and obtains permission to go among Pagan Nations—His voyage to Cadiz—Thence to America..page 8

### CHAPTER III.

Father Junipero is sent to the Missions of Sierra Gorda— The great zeal with which he works — The Mission flourishes............................................... page 14

### CHAPTER IV.

Father Junipero Serra exercises his ministry in different parts of Mexico, before being sent to California.... page 19

### CHAPTER V.

He goes to California with fifteen other missionaries—His works...................................... page 23

## CHAPTER VI.

The expedition by land...... ....................:page 27

## CHAPTER VII.

Discovery of the harbor and bay of San Francisco—Minute details of the expedition and incidents of the voyage, page 34

## CHAPTER VIII.

Father Junipero Serra establishes the first mission in Upper California—What happened then.................page 39

## CHAPTER IX.

Establishment of the Mission of San Carlos at Monterey, .......................................:..............page 47

## CHAPTER X.

Arrival of the Missionaries—Establishment of the Mission of San Antonio—Removal of the San Carlos Mission to Carmel........................... ................ .....page 55

## CHAPTER XI.

Founding of the Mission of San Gabriel—Arrival of six missionaries at San Diego—The port of San Francisco again visited ............................................page 61

## CHAPTER XII.

Journey of Father Junipero to the Capitol of Mexico—Incidents in his travels—Success obtained by his visit..page 69

## CHAPTER XIII.

Exploration by sea to the north of Monterey.......page 75

## CHAPTER XIV.

Apostolic labors of Father Junipero Serra after his return from Mexico—Father Jayme is put to death in his Mission of San Diego............................page 82

## CHAPTER XV.

Father Junipero goes to San Diego—Useless efforts to re-established the Mission—Arrival of troops—The Mission is re-established, and that of San Juan Capistrano founded ............................page 90

## CHAPTER XVI.

Establishment of the Missions of San Francisco and Santa Clara—Wise orders given by the Viceroy—Father Junipero visits these Missions and founds the Pueblo of San Jose, ............................page 94

## CHAPTER XVII.

Father Junipero receives from the Holy See faculties to confirm—He exercises his new powers in Monterey and other missions—New Government—Death of Bucareli—Difficulties............................page 108

## CHAPTER XVIII.

Establishment in the Channel of Santa Barbara—Foundation of San Buenaventura—Sad occurrence in the Rio Colorado............................page 114

# ERRATA.

On page 5, instead of "wa well instructed," should read "was well instructed."

On page 9, instead of "13th of April, 1797," should read "13th of April, 1749."

On page 26, instead of "the caller's consideration," should read "the latter's consideration."

On page 33, instead of "the date of the mission," should read "the date of the missive."

On page 87, instead of "was born," should read "was borne."

## CHAPTER XIX.

Last visit of Fr. Junipero to the missions north and south of Monterey.................................... page 123

## CHAPTER XX.

Exemplary death and imposing funeral of the Ven. Father Junipero Serra—His virtues.................... page 129

## CHAPTER XXI.

Mission of Carmelo, its ruins and its restoration.... page 144

www.ingramcontent.com/pod-product-compliance
Lightning Source LLC
LaVergne TN
LVHW051104080426
835508LV00019B/2054